Send to processing on return

ONE WEEK LOAN

Sto. 4WK LOAN ON
CATALOGUE

1 6 NOV 2007

- 7 DEC 2007
1 0 JAN 2008
- 4 FEB 2008
2 3 APR 2008

- 4 NOV 2011

The Key Concepts

ISSN 1747-6550

The series aims to cover the core disciplines and the key cross-disciplinary ideas across the Humanities and Social Sciences. Each book isolates the key concepts to map out the theoretical terrain across a specific subject or idea. Designed specifically for student readers, each book in the series includes boxed case material, summary chapter bullet points, annotated guides to further reading and questions for essays and class discussion

Forthcoming in this series

Technoculture: The Key Concepts
Debbie Shaw

Design: The Key Concepts
Mark Westgarth and Eleanor Quince

Fashion: The Key Concepts
Jennifer Craik

Food: The Key Concepts
Warren Belasco

Globalization: The Key Concepts
Thomas Hylland Eriksen

New Media: The Key Concepts
Nicholas Gane

Performance: The Key Concepts
Philip Auslander

Photography: The Key Concepts
David Bate

Queer Theory: The Key Concepts
Noreen Giffney

Race: The Key Concepts
C. Richard King

The Body: The Key Concepts
Lisa Blackman

Visual Culture: The Key Concepts
John Lynch

FILM

The Key Concepts

Nitzan Ben-Shaul

Oxford • New York

English edition
First published in 2007 by
Berg

Editorial offices:
First Floor, Angel Court, 81 St Clements Street, Oxford OX4 1AW, UK
175 Fifth Avenue, New York, NY 10010, USA

Library of Congress Cataloging-in-Publication Data

Ben-Shaul, Nitzan S.
    Film : the key concepts / Nitzan Ben-Shaul.
      p. cm.—(The key concepts)
    Includes bibliographical references and index.
    ISBN-13: 978-1-84520-365-8 (cloth)
    ISBN-10: 1-84520-365-8 (cloth)
    ISBN-13: 978-1-84520-366-5 (pbk.)
    ISBN-10: 1-84520-366-6 (pbk.)
  1. Motion pictures. I. Title.

    PN1994.B4147 2007
    791.43—dc22

                                        2006033244

British Library Cataloguing-in-Publication Data

A catalogue record for this book is available from the British Library.

ISBN 978 1 84520 365 8 (Cloth)
        978 1 84520 366 5 (Paper)

Typeset by JS Typesetting Ltd, Porthcawl, Mid Glamorgan.
Printed in the United Kingdom by Biddles Ltd, King's Lynn.

www.bergpublishers.com

To the memory of my mother, may she rest in peace.

CONTENTS

PREFACE

This book is based on various film theory courses I have been giving for the past fifteen years at the Film and Television Department in Tel Aviv University. I would like to thank my students in these courses. Their varied questions and comments helped me to consolidate a presentation of the different theories addressed by the book as clearly as possible. I would also like to thank my colleagues at the department, particularly Dr Anat Zanger, Professor Nurit Gertz and Professor Michal Friedman for their contribution to the organization and teaching of the film theory course of studies in the department.

I thank Tristan Palmer from Berg Publishers, for suggesting this book to me and for his gracious accompaniment of its different stages of production. I also thank the anonymous reviewers of the book for their valuable suggestions.

I especially thank my wife Daphna Cohen Ben-Shaul and my daughters, Noga, Carmel and Guy, for their patience and support.

I dedicate this book to Professor Annette Michelson, my present friend and former doctoral adviser at the Cinema Studies Department in New York University. Thanks to her in-depth seminars I devoted my professional life to the theoretical research of film.

Nitzan Ben-Shaul
Tel Aviv University

INTRODUCTION

Differing from film history, film criticism or filmmaking – activities that deal with specific films in specific historical contexts – film theory strives to offer general ideas on the nature of film and models for film analysis, presumably applicable to every film irrespective of its specific context of production. Beyond the obvious pleasure and reward involved in thinking about this multilayered culturally dominant medium, film theory enriches our viewing. It also aids historians, critics and filmmakers who are by necessity consciously or inadvertently guided by theoretical assumptions in their practice.

Learning about what has been said on the nature of film, on its peculiar signifying processes, on its ideological and psychological effects, or on the ways it can be productively placed within historical, social, spectator or authorial contexts broadens our comprehension of the medium, enriches our viewing, and enhances awareness of the theoretical questions relevant and deserving attention when writing film history, criticizing a film or making one.

This book aims to provide a brief and coherent overview of film theory for beginning readers. It isolates six key concepts in four chapters, through which the main sites in film theory are covered. Each chapter follows the changing conception of the concept addressed through key articles. Some necessary historical guidelines and references to adjacent fields are offered, along with boxed summaries analysing films and bulleted summaries at the end of each chapter to provide beginning students with a map of the field. A section offering questions for essays and class discussions and an annotated bibliography appear at the back of the book.

Each key concept focuses attention on a particular aspect of the medium: 'From the Photogenic to the Simulacrum' addresses the evolving understanding of the relation between film and reality. It opposes the realist version of film as revealing reality through its reproduction, to the formalist conception of film-art as anti-realist. These two opposing views find relief in the postmodern notion of the simulacrum, according to which 'film' and 'reality' are both simulations. 'Film Constructs' focuses on the evolving notion of how films signify. It starts with the semiological and structural comprehension of films as enclosed structures, followed by the poststructural deconstruction of such enclosures, ending with the reconstructive cognitivist position that places signification in the mutual play of film text and the spectator's cognition. 'Dialectic Film Montage' addresses the notion of film's ideological functioning. It traces the comprehension of film as ideology from early constructivist Marxism, to deconstructive neo-Marxism and anti-colonialism, and on to post-Marxism and postcolonialism. 'Imaginary Signifiers/Voyeuristic Pleasures' focuses on the relation between film and the spectator's psyche, dealing with how films offer a generalized spectator voyeuristic pleasures and the reinforcement of his/her sense of self. This is followed by the feminist and queer theory focus upon the diverse voyeuristic pleasures and displeasures offered by films to different genders or to a diversity of sexual sensibilities, concluding with the non-gendered cyborg myth.

In order to address the hotly contested topic of film theory, the book offers a cross-referencing of films and readings across chapters as a way of affirming the flexibility of the categories being set up, leaving them open for emergent concerns. Moreover, while each chapter stands on its own, tracing the historical evolution of each concept to the present, the book shows how ideas/approaches/theorists interact across the last century. This is done through the underlining of an overall homologous evolution across chapters of aligned conceptual comprehensions within different theories, and through dialectically opposing theoretical approaches to each other within and across chapters.

1 FROM THE PHOTOGENIC TO THE SIMULACRUM

INTRODUCTION

The concept of the photogenic in film was developed by French theorist and film-maker Jean Epstein. It concerns the specific nature of the film image. For the different variants of the realist approach to film, the photogenic implies the cine-camera's unique ability to *reveal* hidden dimensions of the photographed object. The formalists rejected this understanding of the term and developed a diametrically opposed conception. For them the photogenic is an aesthetic quality derived solely from film's stylistic *transformations and abstractions* of the recorded images. The Russian formalist Yuri Tynjanov coined the term cinematogenic as a correction to the photogenic. He used the term to imply the peculiar aesthetics of film that derive from its transmutation of reality resembling qualities, qualities that in themselves had no artistic merit in his view.

The realist/formalist debate as it evolved around the concept of the photogenic has a long art-theory pedigree. It concerns different approaches to the purpose, value and function of art. While realists conceived art as striving to reveal the truth about the world or its beauty through imitation of its surface appearance, formalists maintained that art should distance itself from nature and express the human capacity for abstraction. Both positions share the premise that there is no effective way to commingle the aesthetic values found in nature with those of human-made art. As phrased by art theorist and psychologist Rudolph Arnheim:

> There is a decisive difference between things of nature and works of art... In the visual arts ... form is applied to a material by external influence. In fact, the artist tends to avoid highly organized materials such as crystals or plants. The art of arranging flowers is hybrid because it subjects organic shape to human order... Kracauer has pointed out that in photography highly defined compositional form falsifies the medium... Artistic shape is made, whereas

> organic shape is grown... The shape of a seashell or a leaf is the external
> manifestation of the inner forces that produced the object.[1]

The formalist position came to the fore with the artistic ferment of the modernist movement that emerged at the end of the nineteenth century and the beginnings of the twentieth century with movements such as impressionism, expressionism and cubism, each trying in its own fashion to break away from the traditional commitment of the arts to imitate reality as it is normatively perceived. The concomitant advent of film generated a heated debate over its value as an art form. It brought forth a hidden dichotomy between two widespread premises concerning art's essence – namely, that each artistic form fashions its own peculiar materials (music fashions sounds, poetry fashions words, painting fashions colour, etc.) and that art strives towards abstraction. Hence, for the formalists, art's struggle for abstraction was bound by definition to encounter strong resistance from the film's 'material' given its technological, automatic and highly mimetic way of recording reality. For them, the medium was anti-aesthetic according to its material and hence somewhat limited in its artistic potential. On the other hand, the same presumption about each art form's peculiar material base brought those who saw film as a new art form to call for a new aesthetic, realist in its nature and befitting film's peculiar material base.

The dialectic between these founding conceptions of film as art frame to a large extent the aesthetic debates surrounding the medium and the motivations provided for its evolution. Some, like André Bazin, described the evolution of film as a constant struggle to reaffirm its commitment to reproducing reality and reduce to a minimum what he perceived as the medium's non-cinematic tendency for abstract fabrications. Others, like Tynjanov,[2] saw the medium's aesthetic evolution as striving towards abstraction through overcoming its debasing faculty of reproduction. This dialectic is also evident in most film histories, which usually open with the opposition between the early documentary filmmaking of the Lumière brothers and the cinematic tricks of their contemporary Georges Méliès, a magician turned filmmaker. For instance, the Lumière brothers' documentary film *Arrival of a Train at La Ciotat* (1896) consisted of one stationary shot showing a train arriving from the screen's background to its foreground at a station and the passengers getting off, whereas Méliès fantastic film *A Trip to the Moon* (1902) mixed animation with recorded images, stop-motion, superimpositions and other cinematographic effects.

These founding conceptions haunted each other, failing to account for film aesthetics whenever each ignored the other. Realist positions failed to provide a comprehensive account of the complex conventions of editing, film metaphors or narrative that construct even the most realist of films, while formalist positions failed to account for the complex documentary import of film images and sounds.

The postmodern revolution offered to break down this long-held tension between realist and formalist conceptions of film. Baudrillard's notion of *simulacra* shattered the traditional distinction between the object as origin for the image simulating it. Perceiving this distinction as arbitrary and unwarranted, he claimed that the simulated image (e.g. film) does not originate from something beyond it (such as 'reality') but precedes or even originates what it presents. The concept of simulacrum implied that film was neither a reproduction of reality nor its artistic abstraction. For Baudrillard reality is not an origin for an image re-presenting it since 'reality' is always-already an image or a simulation. This engendered a conception of film as one among other fluid successions of images and sounds whose tagging as 'documentary', 'fictional' or 'artistic' referred to nothing else but different and equally valid modes of simulation.

The following sections consider the major realist and formalist comprehensions of the photogenic in film followed by a discussion of the notion of film as simulacrum.

I REALIST APPROACHES

A major premise underlining most realist approaches to the photogenic is that film is a medium with a peculiar realist capacity to bring forth hidden or overlooked aspects of reality through its moving, audiovisual recordings of appearances. This is derived from the medium's *way* of producing images and sounds. Differing from even the most accurate of paintings, film images result from a mechanical process of reproduction without the need for human intervention in the recording process itself. This process results in moving images and sounds that resemble better than any other medium the way humans see and hear their surroundings.

As will be seen, the way in which film produces its images and sounds is also the ground upon which critics of photogenic realism base their aesthetic, structural, cognitive, psychological or ideological reservations. In focusing upon the realist claim that film is better situated to go beyond appearances merely by its mode of reproduction, these critics consider film realism to lack aesthetic worth and cognitive purpose, or as a psychologically misleading and ideologically harmful conception of film.

1.1 PHOTOGENIC TRUTH IN FILM

The term 'photogenic' in relation to film was used in the 1920s by Jean Epstein, a leading early French impressionist avant-garde filmmaker and theoretician. As discussed by Stuart Liebman in his study of Epstein, the term encapsulated his conception of film as art as well as his epistemological premises. For Epstein the photogenic was a revelation or enhancement, through cinematography, of hidden qualities stemming from the object photographed. In his view, film's capacity to reveal such qualities was not restricted to the mechanical reproduction of the object by photography, but was also found in the film's rendering of photographed objects and events in motion, revealing rhythms hidden from our daily perception. Epstein's belief that these qualities were hidden from normal perception led him to try to reveal them through cinematic devices such as varying lenses, changes of camera distance and angle, the shifting of the camera's recording speed from fast to slow motion, and the shifting of editing rhythms. This can be evidenced in some of his films, particularly in *Coeur Fidele* (1923) and *The Fall of the House of Usher* (1928).

What drove Epstein was the type of knowledge about the world offered by film. He distinguished epistemologically between intellectual and emotional forms of knowledge. While the intellect asks how the world operates and tries to decipher the laws governing nature, emotional knowledge ponders about the world's existence and strives to gain such knowledge through intuition or direct unmediated evidence. As Epstein wrote, 'knowledge through feeling is immediate... Whereas we grope our way toward scientific understanding, feeling gushes forth insight'.[3] Probably influenced by the writings of French philosopher Henri Bergson, who argued that we intuitively sense the existence of things and that the basis of this is motion, Epstein suggested that a crucial component of emotional knowledge had to do with motion. Hence film's shifting images in motion evoked the emotional mode of knowledge. Moreover, argued Epstein, since emotional knowledge is based on emotions that by definition cannot be rendered verbally, the suspension of verbal articulation in silent film further encourages emotional knowledge. Thus, for Epstein, film's capacity to render silent images of recorded objects and events in motion, turned it into a unique art form capable of enhancing emotional knowledge.

Moreover, silent film was for Epstein *the* art form of the new modern era. This was because it catered to what he termed a *lyrosophical* way of knowing that was peculiar to the era, described by Epstein as a 'kind of passive state of the brain; there is enough distraction, that is to say engagement, to allow the senses freely to record or not the movements of the external world, and there is also disquiet enough in this torpor so that the attention emerges at the slightest unexpected noise.'[4] Epstein believed that this lyrosophical state of partial awareness, stemming from the constant fatigue in which modern people find themselves due to the dizzying pace of life dictated by modern technology, brought humans closer to emotionally knowing the world because it neutralized intellectual knowledge. Hence, silent film befitted the lyrosophical episteme both because it neutralized intellectual knowledge in its being silent, and because of its large amount of visual stimuli, provided by its shifting images in motion.

Epstein saw a direct relation between the photogenic revelation of film, motion and emotional knowledge. Hence, the photogenicity of the world, revealed *through* motion, offered emotional rather than intellectual knowledge.

Thus the photogenic does not merely reveal hidden qualities, but these qualities can only be known emotionally, in a direct, intellectually unmediated way. Therefore, the photogenic addresses the visual sense through images in motion: 'Photogenic mobility is simultaneously movement in space and time. It can therefore be said that the photogenic aspect of things is a result of its variations in space-time.'[5]

In such manner the photogenic reveals to the eye of the beholder hidden qualities in matter as well as the personality of the photographed people. As he writes, 'What is *photogenie*? I shall call photogenic those aspects of things, of beings and of souls whose moral stature is enhanced by their cinematographic reproduction.'[6]

In sum, for Epstein, filmmakers are to try to bring forth the elusive photogenic qualities of figured objects and people through all available cinematic devices (particularly close-up shots that bring us emotionally closer to the character or object figured, while also 'abstracting' their essence by decontextualizing them from their surroundings). Shifting film images evoke the lyrosophical mode that offers viewers a direct knowledge of the essence of things, events and people.

The documentary photogenic core embedded in filmed images was of ongoing concern to film theoreticians. Even the 1960s' semiological approaches, which considered the system of sign-conventions in the medium as bearing the full import of its meaning, could not avoid its documentary import, which in turn threatened the legitimacy of their complex delineation of film conventions. Roland Barthes for example, constantly returned to what he perceived to be a photographic paradox: On the one hand photographs call upon us to derive a meaning that semiology can fully explain by relating its various aspects to different sign systems such as detecting symbols, references to previous artistic compositions, or clearly articulated ideological positions. On the other hand, there was for Barthes something in every photographed object that evaded semiological explanation. This became evident for him in the shocking or 'traumatic' effect that photographed images of atrocities have on us, images that arrest our ongoing chains of signification.[7] This documentary import, which seems to be a variant of Epstein's photogenic, returns the viewer to an unmediated, direct experience of the photographed event. Another recent impressive revitalization of Epstein's conception of the uncovering of the photogenic through movement in film (as well as its relation to the philosophy of Bergson) can be found in the extensive writings of Gilles Deleuze on cinema. For Deleuze, the moving film image is not an image *of* something but it *is* that something *as* image, knowable through affect.

1.2 FILM AS TRUTH MACHINE

The positions entertained by Epstein were strongly criticized by early Marxist theoreticians and filmmakers. For them, notions such as Epstein's photogenic truth, knowable through aesthetic-emotional unmediated knowledge were nothing but an idealization and mystification of reality. Far from revealing any truth about the world, its apparent mystery was lauded and positioned as unreachable to human knowledge.[8] Moreover, the mystification embedded in emotional aesthetics blurred people's capacity to realize their real situation in the real world and aided the continuation of their material exploitation.

Notwithstanding this opposition to emotional aesthetics, early Marxists of the 1920s shared Epstein's belief in the capacity of film to reveal truth given its way of reproduction. The documentary filmmaker Dziga Vertov was the strongest proponent of this position. While calling for the separation of art from film, since art was a lie that blinded people to reality, Vertov, like Epstein, saw film as a 'truth machine' due to its mechanical way of reproducing reality. While his notion of truth did not stem from the medium's emotional-aesthetic qualities but from its 'scientific' attributes, he also called for film's decoding or revealing of the dynamics driving manifest appearances. Moreover, Vertov shared Epstein's conception of the film apparatus as capable of enhancing human sensual faculties, calling for the revelation of truth through all the devices allowed by the medium (slow and fast motion, split screens, close-ups, editing, etc.). However, unlike Epstein he aimed at deciphering society's class structure in its relation to the means of production as these are manifest in daily life, through the 'scientific' arrangement (i.e. editing) of 'truth' pieces (i.e. documentary shots).[9]

Vertov's attitude towards truth in film reverberates in Walter Benjamin's 1930s' theses. Like Vertov, Benjamin saw in the attempt to reveal through the photogenic some hidden mystery, which he termed an object or a person's 'aura', a faked ritual.[10] Also, like Vertov, Benjamin thought of film as a truth machine potentially revealing scientific-political aspects of social life. As he wrote:

> By Close-ups of the things around us, by focusing on hidden details of familiar objects, by exploring commonplace milieus under the ingenious guidance of the camera, the film, on the one hand, extends our comprehension of the necessities which rule our lives; on the other hand, it manages to assure us of an immense and unexpected field of action ... Evidently a different nature opens itself to the camera that opens to the naked eye – if only because an unconsciously penetrated space is substituted for a space consciously explored by man.[11]

1.3 PHOTOGENIC BEAUTY IN FILM

Differing from both Epstein's and Vertov's theories of film as revealing truth, the French theoretician André Bazin developed a very influential realist-aesthetic theory of the medium in the 1950s. According to Bazin, film's calling was to reveal the world's beauty to the eyes and ears of cinemagoers. His theory developed from an acceptance of the premise that aesthetic values are either natural or cultural but cannot effectively be both. This led him to try to establish a film aesthetic that would distinguish it from other art forms because of the automatic and mechanical way films reproduce reality. The titles of two of Bazin's seminal essays reveal the problem stemming from this position. Hence, in 'The Ontology of the Photographic Image'[12] Bazin tried to establish an aesthetic of film based on its unique way of reproduction, demanding that filmmakers reveal the world's beauty. However, in his second essay, 'The Evolution of the Language of Cinema',[13] he tried to come to terms with what apparently disturbs natural beauty, that is, the processes of film articulation necessarily imposed from the 'outside' on natural beauty. Bazin's thesis concerning this problem founded his realist film aesthetic.

In 'The Ontology of the Photographic Image' Bazin developed a theory of the evolution of art to ground his conception of film's peculiar realist aesthetic. He argued that beside the struggle to form an expression of human spirituality, art was always committed to fulfil an irrational human craving to safeguard the world's constantly vanishing being, a craving he called 'our obsession with realism'.[14] He found traces of this in the ancient Egyptians' practice of mummification. Bazin found these two impulses to be balanced in medieval religious art in that images resemble the objects depicted but are not committed to their exact reproduction. This allowed artists to express their subjective or spiritual conception. However, he went on, the fourteenth-century invention of linear perspective in the arts broke this delicate balance. This was because by allowing artists to render a deceitful exact copy of appearances, perspective forced them to satisfy the primordial psychological craving to safeguard the world's vanishing being. Hence, the invention of perspective led most artists to forgo the expression of their inner vision, offering instead a deceitful reproduction. However claimed Bazin, the 'sin' of perspective was 'redeemed' by the invention of photography.[15]

Photographic reproduction laid bare the illusion and deception practised by the plastic arts through linear perspective, and freed the plastic arts from their commitment to satisfy the viewer's psychological craving to mummify being. It freed artists to express their inner soul abstractly because the photograph took the role of satisfying the human craving for reality's mummification, given its humanly unmediated, automatic and superior imprint or 'fingerprint' of the reality reproduced.

Film went even further than photography by mummifying the passage of time and movement in space. Hence, even a poorly rendered photograph or film shot seems to offer more convincing evidence of the existence of what it portrays than any exact copy obtained through painting or sculpture. Nevertheless, for Bazin, the freeing of the plastic arts from the need to offer a resemblance of reality did not mean that photography and cinematography were artless. On the contrary, it meant that this new medium called for a different aesthetic stemming from its unique power of reproduction. As Bazin wrote:

> All the arts are based on the presence of man, only photography derives an advantage from his absence. Photography affects us like a phenomenon in nature, like a flower or a snowflake whose vegetable or earthly origins are an inseparable part of their beauty...[16] Those categories of *resemblance* which determine the species *photographic* image likewise, then, determine the character of its aesthetic as distinct from that of painting... The aesthetic qualities of photography are to be sought in its power to lay bear the realities. It is not for me to separate off, in the complex fabric of the objective world, here a reflection on a damp sidewalk, there the gesture of a child. Only the impassive lens, stripping its object of all those ways of seeing it, those piled up preconceptions, that spiritual dust and grime with which my eyes have covered it, is able to present it in all its virginal purity to my attention and consequently to my love.[17]

Bazin's belief in the unique power and function of photography and film to reveal the world's beauty to the eyes of the beholder implied a problem. His calling to filmmakers to neutralize their world-view in order for the 'world' to imprint its aesthetic beauty on the screen was paradoxical. This was because the filmed 'world' is always humanely mediated and structured by the very act of framing, camera angle or editing. Aware of this contradiction, Bazin concluded his essay on the ontology of the photographic image by saying that 'On the other hand, of course, cinema is also a language.'[18]

In 'The Evolution of the Language of Cinema' Bazin tackled the problem and suggested a cinematic articulation that remained loyal to film's aesthetic-realist calling. In his view, the cardinal division in film art was between 'Those directors who put their faith in the image and those who put their faith in reality. By "image" I here mean ... everything that the representation on the screen adds to the object there represented..., [additions] that relate to the plastics of the image and those that relate to the resources of montage, which after all is simply the ordering of images in time'.[19] Hence, filmmakers who derived the meanings of their films not from the qualities stemming from the photographed reality but from their 'violating' this reality by adding theatrical decor and painterly compositions, or by forging meaning primarily from what lies in between the shots through their editing and juxtaposition, missed the realist-aesthetic nature of the medium.

Among these violators of film aesthetics he mentioned the practice of some German expressionist filmmakers who distorted the photographed image by using theatrical and painterly artificial decor. This is clearly evident in Robert Wiene's film *The Cabinet of Dr Caligari* (1919) where the characters wear heavy, accentuated make-up and move within a painted landscape. Others deplored by Bazin included Soviet filmmakers such as Eisenstein and Vertov, who considered the single film shot's value and meaning to derive from its juxtaposition to other shots rather than from the slice of reality it reproduced. What he had in mind can be seen in Vertov's *Man with a Movie Camera*. The film, although composed solely from documentary shots, conveys its meaning not from the brief shot's content but from the shot's decontextualization from the locale where it was taken and its recontextualization through complex juxtapositions to other brief shots in a dazzling rhythmic editing. It is safe to presume that Bazin would also have deplored the *seamless editing* initiated by Griffith and dominant in American filmmaking. He would have considered the latter's attempt at imparting an illusion of uninterrupted flow through tricks of editing (such as cuts in motion or maintaining eye-line matches across shots) as similar in principle to the tricking of the eye used by the plastic arts through linear perspective. Although Bazin conceded that these filmmakers developed different film styles and genres, these were not cinematic since they violated the aesthetic import of the mummified images.

As against these, Bazin mentioned various directors whom he claimed were driven by a realist aesthetic derived from the imprint of the recorded reality on film. A summary of Bazin's description of these filmmakers' aesthetics reveals the cinematic compositions considered by him as essential to any realist film aesthetic. Hence, in describing Flaherty's poetic documentary *Nanook of the North* (1922), Bazin was fascinated by Flaherty's lengthy uncut rendition in long shot of Nanook waiting for and eventually catching a seal in the snow, since it caused the viewer to experience the passage of time aesthetically. Likewise, he found in F. W. Murnau's expressionist films a realist poetic rendering of the notion of 'destiny'. This can be seen in an uncut long shot in *Nosferatu* (1922) showing the slow approach of a ship carrying Nosferatu the vampire in his coffin to the dock of a medieval town. When writing on Erich von Stroheim's films, Bazin addressed his use of long close-up shots whose length gradually 'revealed' the filmed character's inner 'cruelty of being', a process he compared to the breaking of a suspect under intense interrogation. A good example of what Bazin has in mind is Carl Theodor Dryer's film *The Passion of Joan of Arc* (1928), which is mostly comprised of a series of long, grainy close-ups of the actress Falconnetti, whose tortured silent face conveys Joan of Arc's mounting despair in face of her executioners. Throughout the shot's uninterrupted length, revealing through its uncut duration the beauty of the passage of time (Flaherty), the sense of 'destiny'

(Murnau) or the revelation of inner feelings (Von Stroheim), Bazin emphasized the use of deep-focus lenses that enhanced the viewer's experience of the world's three-dimensionality and depth, by maintaining the foreground and background portions of the shot in focus. He found Jean Renoir's use of deep-focus shots particularly fascinating, since Renoir's 'search after composition in depth … is based on a respect for the continuity of dramatic space and, of course, of its duration.'[20] As pointed out to me by Annette Michelson, Renoir's obsession with depth can be seen in a shot from his film *The Little Match Girl* (1928) where he shoots from one window the window of a building opposite; suddenly a box of matches thrown from below floats into the shot and swirls in the air, opening up the space between the buildings (earlier unnoticed because of the flat two-dimensional screen).

For Bazin, Orson Welles's *Citizen Kane* (1941) brought aesthetic realism to un-precedented heights through its use of single long deep-focused shots to convey an entire sequence. Welles's deep-focused one-shot sequences covered an entire dramatic event without recourse to cutting, thereby preserving the event's duration while enhancing spatial depth. An emblematic example of this strategy can be seen in the scene from the film where Kane the child is being given away by his mother to the guardianship of a financier named Thatcher. The whole scene is conveyed in one long deep-focused shot in which we see the mother in the foreground discussing the arrangement with Thatcher while in the background, through a window, we see little Kane happily playing in the snow, unaware of the transaction that will change the course of his life forever.

From Bazin's fascination with the long deep-focused shot and his rejection of 'artificial' framing and editing we may deduce that his approach to framing conceived

---

One-Shot Sequences in Angelopolous's *Landscape in the Mist* and Snow's *Wavelength*

Later elaborations of one-shot sequences can be found in the films of Greek director Theo Angelopolous. In his *Landscape in the Mist* (1988) there is a scene where a truck-driver rapes a girl he gave a ride to in the back of his truck. Angelopolous conveys this event through one lengthy shot that starts with a view from afar of the back of the parked truck, showing the driver slowly stepping out of the cabin, climbing into the darkened back of the truck where we know the girl is, and stepping out after a while. The camera then starts to move in slowly towards the darkened space and as it reaches a closer view the girl is shown tumbling down out of the truck and walking slowly away towards the road. The event is powerfully conveyed by the slow movement of the camera towards the truck. It literally emblematizes Bazin's idea of the mystery of depth in

of the shot as a window showing part of a vaster reality rather than as a self-enclosed 'artificial' composition, whereas editing devices such as cuts and dissolves were conceived of as necessary transitions in time and space between slices of reality rather than as 'artificial' stylistic or rhythmical juxtapositions. A good idea of what Bazin had in mind in terms of framing and editing can be seen in Pier Paolo Pasolini's film *Accatone* (1961), where he conveys a sense of using inattentive cutting across 'slice of reality' shots, achieved by sparse and seemingly sporadic cuts between lengthy long shots of the same locale, as when he follows in a few shots a group of noisy, low-class boys, slowly climbing up from a river, showing wretched-looking dwellings spread in the natural scenery, whose expanse and depth are emphasized. This realist-aesthetic approach recurred in many other neo-realist films such as Roberto Rosselini's *Paisan* (1946) and Vittorio De Sica's *Bicycle Thieves* (1948). In these films, the use of what appears to the viewer as inattentive cutting between deep-focused shots was often through dissolves that imparted a notion of time condensation rather than disjunction.

Hence, the long deep-focused take, enhancing the passage of time; the fullness and three-dimensionality of objects shot in close-up; the depth and expanse of space in long shots; and the minimal use of editing, conceived of as a transition between slices of reality, were the basic tropes considered by Bazin to be powerful and authentic film articulations. This was because these tropes satisfied in his view the spectators' craving for the mummification of being while positioning them in such a way that they could aesthetically experience the flowing passage of objective time, the world's 'depth' and 'ambiguity,' and the gradually manifested yet mysterious inner being of the pre-recorded event, object or character.

---

space. Moreover, the narrative process of revelation is embedded in this one, slow, continuous camera movement despite the fact that, or rather because, the camera never shows what went on.

This intense sense of a process of narrative revelation through one shot was explored by the avant-garde American filmmaker Michael Snow in his film *Wavelength* (1967). The film consists of a single, 45-minute-long tracking shot with the camera slowly crossing an almost empty New York loft towards a meaningless black and white photograph of a sea wave hung on the opposite wall.

1.4 CRITIQUES OF PHOTOGENIC BEAUTY IN FILM

Let us begin with a discussion of the world-view embedded in Bazin's film aesthetic. In different places Bazin emphasized that out of the continuous long deep-focused framing of reality the 'mystery' of a character or of spatial depth was gradually revealed. Bazin described this result as 'metaphysical' whereby 'depth of focus reintroduces ambiguity into the structure of the image... The uncertainty in which we find ourselves as to the spiritual key or the interpretation we should put on the film is built into the very design of the image.'[21] Also, as has been shown, the viewer's exposure to the world's mystery through recorded 'fingerprints' implied that in authentic filmmaking the film's artist is nature or the world and not the people who made the film, whose main function was to help the world deliver itself aesthetically. Finally, Bazin tended to treat photographic and cinematographic ontology in metaphysical, often religious terms, imparting a kind of holy power to these images. This comes through in the conflation he made between image and object whereby the photograph 'shares, by virtue of the very process of its becoming, the being of the model of which it is the reproduction; it is the model'.[22] Moreover, in his use of the term 'violence' to describe 'artificial' manipulations of photographs, in his contempt for the 'tricks' of linear perspective, in his use of terms such as 'virginal purity' to describe the photographed image, in calling the invention of linear perspective a 'sin' and the advent of photography a 'redemption' from that sin, a religious world-view surfaced in Bazin's writings.

Indeed, Bazin's aesthetic realism has often been used explicitly to depict a spiritual, metaphysical reality that commingles real and spiritual worlds. This is evident, for instance, in Wim Wender's film *Wings of Desire* (1987). By using Bazinian-type long deep-focused shots in a floating movement, Wenders conveyed the point of view of two angels, imparting the notion that the essence of the reality depicted was spiritual. Particularly impressive is the series of floating long shots in Berlin's city library in which one of the angels is shown walking unseen among the library visitors while hearing their inner thoughts. The scene's highlight comes when the angel picks up the tangible spiritual counterpart of a pen lying on a table while the 'material' pen itself remains unmoved.

Bazin tended to read metaphysical meanings into films on account of socio-political implications. As noted by MacBean, in his comments on Luis Buñuel's film *Land without Bread* (1932), Bazin was fascinated by Buñuel's documentary images of the poor inhabitants of the remote Spanish town of Las Hurdes, finding in these an abstract spiritual expression of the wretched destiny of humanity and of human suffering. He overlooked, however, Buñuel's harsh criticism of the Spanish authorities and of the church, blamed in the film for the miserable situation of people whose hunger bred hereditary retardation.[23]

Bazin's film-realist aesthetic was criticized by 1960s' neo-Marxist and psychoanalytic film theorists. Their critique was based on the acceptance of Bazin's film aesthetic premise that viewers are positioned in such a way that they believe that the film being played is real. Accepting this premise, they attacked Bazin on the grounds that the represented 'reality' was actually a powerful ideological (neo-Marxists) or imaginary (psychoanalysts) projection, imparting the notion that reality's essence is spiritual and reinforcing the viewers' deceitful perception of their own selves as spiritual. Henceforth, they insisted, the best thing films could do was to deconstruct this imaginary illusion and disjoin the illusory cinematic continuum so as to force viewers to be constantly aware of the film's ideological manipulations. Differing from early Marxists such as Vertov, these theoreticians rejected the truth-value of any film images whatsoever. These were, to use Althusser's term, 'always-already' imaginary ideological projections determined by the capitalist mode of production.[24]

Cognitivists of the 1980s and 1990s rejected Bazin's premise that realist films caused viewers to believe in the reality represented. Therefore they also rejected the neo-Marxist and psychoanalytic critiques of Bazin. According to cognitivists, viewers are active agents processing the projected film data out of constant awareness that the film is a reproduction rather than reality itself. Noel Carroll, for example, rejected the widely accepted notion of the 'suspension of disbelief' upon which many theoreticians based their explanations of the viewers' belief in, and consequent emotional involvement with, a movie. Why, asked Carroll, do spectators remain seated and not escape the theatre when they see a roaring lion on screen? In fact, claimed Carroll, people can get emotionally involved when entertaining 'what if' thoughts without needing to believe in the actual existence of such thoughts. Hence, I can think and visualize someone dear to me on the brink of jumping off a cliff and get emotionally agitated without needing to believe that the deed happened. Moreover, asked Carroll, how can a person willingly suspend his disbelief? Can I make myself willingly believe that $1 + 1 = 3$? Therefore Carroll rejected Bazin's premise concerning the spectators' belief in the reality portrayed by film, viewing this as a misunderstanding of the spectators' active cognitive processes.[25]

The 1990s' cognitivist critique of film realism was akin to the 1920s' film-formalist position. Both shared the notion that film realism was simply one cinematic style among others. Formalists even considered film realism to be a poor cinematic style since it did not strive for the abstraction they demanded of art. Let us turn to the formalist notion of the photogenic in film.

2 FORMALIST APPROACHES TO ART

The basic principles of the formalist approach to film derive from their general conception of art. Formalists contended that art is an autonomous human activity having its own essence and should be discussed in terms relevant to its essence. Therefore, conceptions of works of art derived from extra-artistic contexts such as trying to learn about history or about an artist's psychology or biography from the work of art are irrelevant to art. According to the Russian formalist Victor Shklovsky,

> art exists (so) that one may recover the sensation of life; it exists to make one feel things, to make the stone *stony*... The technique of art is to make objects 'unfamiliar,' to make forms difficult, to increase the difficulty and length of perception because the process of perception is an aesthetic end in itself. Art is a way of experiencing the artfulness of an object; the object itself is not important.[26]

Hence, art's essence resides in the human abstraction of content through form, irrespective of the reality function of such a process. Thus, a man drowning would probably cry 'help!' since, were he to poetize his words, those around him would probably stop and listen to him rather than help him out. What is important in art as opposed to daily functional activities is that art draws attention to its forms. It does so by different devices 'estranging' familiar objects from customary perceptions (e.g. a huge oblique close-up of one hair). In this way, perceivers of art are forced to pay attention to the object's formation and to their act of perception as they try to figure out the object.

Formalists argued that the process whereby contents are transformed to be artistic consists of shifting their real or natural motivations towards artistic motivations. Therefore, mimetic arts were considered by the formalists to be inferior arts since their composition was motivated by an attempt to mimic the shape of real things rather than by the artistic struggle towards abstraction.

Composition and style in art were considered by the formalists to be the major artistic functions responsible for forging a work's artistic context. The Russian formalist Tynjanov explained this by showing how in Gogol's short story 'The Nose' (1836), through a compositional and stylistic shaping of words, the reader accepts as plausible a nose that is detached from a body and that can talk, think and move around.[27]

Furthermore, just as art's general essence resides in the shaping of matter towards abstraction, so each artistic medium has its own specific essence in that its abstracting formal devices develop from its specific means of production. As the formalist Boris Kazanskij put it, 'The specific properties of any art form whatever, we are taught by the contemporary science of art-study, must be sought in its manner of execution, i.e. in its material technological basis. This in turn conditions both its entire system of devices and the full range of variations in its styles.'[28] Thus music shapes sounds towards abstraction through musical instruments, poetry shapes words through writing, painting shapes colours through brushes and canvas, and theatre shapes the living, present human being through acting, stage and decor. Attempts to shape the matter of one art form according to abstracting devices developed through the means of production of other arts were perceived by formalists as alien to the art form. Thus, trying to use compositions stemming from painting or poetry to shape the living human being in theatre renders poor theatre, just as trying to understand a play through the real history it alludes to renders a poor understanding of the play.

2.1 THE FORMALIST APPROACH TO THE PHOTOGENIC

Film posed a challenge to the early 1920s' formalists since it implied a contradiction between two of their major art premises: that which concerned the specificity of each art form's means of production and that which called for abstraction through these specific means. Although they saw in film the advent of a new art form before their very eyes and began studying its artistic potential, their premise concerning art's struggle to abstraction through its means of production raised questions regarding the new medium's artistic potential, given film's technological automatic rendering of exact reproductions. Moreover, the recorded results were too bound to the recorded object, making it difficult for the artist to shift their realist motivation towards stylistic abstraction.

In a series of collected essays published in 1927 under the title *Poetika Kino* (The Poetics of Film) several Russian formalists applied the formalist aesthetic premises to different aspects of the film medium.[29] The most comprehensive and groundbreaking approach can be found in Yuri Tynjanov's article 'On the Foundations of Cinema'.[30]

Tynjanov opened with a rejection of the realist and naturalist approaches to film. While film's mechanical reproduction aroused excitement, in his view this excitement had nothing to do with art. He compared this to prehistoric man's attribution of magical qualities to a leopard head painted on the blade that killed his prey. What was important for Tynjanov was not the painting's resemblance to the prey or its attendant magical power, but the fact that in time the painting may have gone through a process of abstraction to become the tribe's symbol, indicating the emergence of language and art. As he wrote, 'a real leopard will not result anyway, and ... art has little use for real leopards.'[31]

Art was defined by Tynjanov as antithetical to reality. He therefore considered photographic reproduction to be artless since in his mind it resists abstraction and focuses the viewer's attention upon the reality content of the photograph, bringing forth its daily, ordinary perception. Tynjanov's anti-naturalism led him to develop a two-phased theory of film art making. His theory was based on the still photograph as the film's basic material, conceived of as nothing but a pale and distorted copy of its recorded object. This distortion was the result of the camera lenses, angle, distance, exposure and framing, which form, reality wise, mistaken relations between the objects included in the frame. These distortions, however, while having the potential to forge an artistic context, do not add up to a shift in the viewer's attribution of naturalistic motivations to the photograph. Hence the photograph was for him bound forever to the object it necessarily distorted. However, these initial photographic distortions allow the filmmaker to forge an artistic context by interrelating them, since the film is based on a series of still photographs and on their editing. This interrelation frees the recorded object from its naturalist context and its being bound to one spot, and necessarily places it within a new context. Hence, Tynjanov preferred the term cinematogenicity over photogenicity, since the latter term drew attention to the reproducing qualities of photographs rather than to their abstract aesthetic ones, located only on the film and not in the single photograph. According to Tynjanov, this necessary new film context can become artistic if the original distortions found in each still photograph are formed into a calculated style:

> Cinema was born of photography. The umbilical cord between them was cut at the moment that cinema perceived itself as art... Photography... surreptitiously deforms the object. Deformation (in photography) is permitted, but on one condition: that the primary focus on verisimilitude is maintained... But cinema has a different focus, and photography's 'shortcoming' becomes cinema's virtue, its aesthetic feature.[32]

Hence, Tynjanov and other formalists rejected the realist claim that the photogenic refers to a quality existing in the photographed object, revealed through the photograph. For them, the aesthetic quality of photographed objects, which is the only concern of art, is a result of the way these are transmuted by the devices of film and has nothing to do with the real object photographed or any hidden quality it might have. Any object can be aesthetic since this is a function of the stylistic transmutation of photographed objects. Film photogenicity, or rather cinematogenicity, frees the transmuted objects from their being bound to one place, as in the still photograph, and allows through editing the swift shift of space and time as well as the latter's abstraction. As he writes, 'Unity of place is not a problem for cinema, its only problem is the unity of camera angle and lighting... Objects are not in and of themselves photogenic. They are made photogenic by camera angle and lighting.

The concept of "photogenie" must, therefore, yield altogether to the concept of cinematogeny.'[33]

From this Tynjanov reached the conclusion that the two main devices specific to the art of film are the cinematogenic (i.e. the stylistic transmutation of objects within shots due to the cine-camera's 'distortions') and the montage (the 'mounting' or editing of film shots). These devices shift the photographed object's naturalistic motivation towards an artistic one.

While the cinematogenic shifts a figured object's meaning away from naturalistic motivations towards an artistic context within the shot, montage stylistically interrelates the film shots allowing for the 'semantic correlativity of the visible world ... rendered by means of its stylistic transformation.'[34]

He therefore rejected as artless the realist exaltation of the perceived living person or inanimate object in photography. The photographed person or object can function in naturalistic or artistic contexts just as the same word can offer information in a newspaper or figure in a poem. 'The visible world is presented in cinema not as such, but in its semantic correlativity... The visible man and the visible thing constitute an element of cinematic art only when they serve as a semantic sign.'[35] He therefore rejected the notion of similitude in film typecasting. According to him the choice of actor is to be derived from his/her relation to other actors or objects and not from an ordinary real context. His anti-naturalism led him to also suspect motion in film,

> Motion in cinema exists either to *motivate the camera angle* through the point of view of a moving character, or as a means of *characterizing* the person (gesture); it may also be used to *alter the relationship* between people and things ... motion in cinema exists not in and of itself, but as a certain semantic sign... (Motion within a shot as an element of cinema has, in general, been highly exaggerated; hustle and bustle no matter what is tiring).[36]

Tynjanov found particular interest in close-ups, which (once rid of naturalistic motivations such as intimacy through closeness) detach part of an object from its whole (such as a head or hand from the body), allowing filmmakers to create abstractions such as symbols and metaphors. In Pudovkin's film *Mother* (1926), for example, a long shot of a rallying crowd is cut to a close-up of a hand waving a red flag against the sky, coming to symbolize the spirit and direction of revolution. He also highly valued the device of dissolve because of its capacity to articulate simultaneity, as well as its abstracting the very notion of motion as is often the case in dance films. However, the film's illusion of three-dimensionality, if emphasized, disturbed the abstracting potential of dissolves because the device appears to violate natural law in its commingling of three-dimensional objects, thus generating eerie, artless sensations in spectators. (This claim that dissolves create eerie effects may seem outdated, but we can imagine what he has in mind in face of the eerie effects often produced by the present use of digital morphing, through which objects seem to violate natural law in their seamless mutation).

Finally, Tynjanov raised doubts as to the art value for film of adding colour and sound since these may tilt the medium once again towards naturalism and realism. It should be pointed out, however, that Tynjanov's fears are groundless insofar as his theory goes. As Jakobson has pointed out, films can abstract sound just as they abstract images. In fact, filmmakers use sounds and colours extensively as abstracting devices. Hence, Godard's opening shots in *Contempt* (1963) are tinted in red and blue, symbolizing the colours of the French flag. Likewise, his widespread use of asynchronous sound and image relations draws attention to film's manipulation of sound–image synchrony, as in a scene in *Le Chinoise* (1967) where the characters add a romantic musical score on a gramophone to accompany the repetition of a conversation they just had, laying bare how the meaning of the scene changes into a melodramatic interchange once the musical score is added.

Just as Tynjanov rejected naturalist motivations for film shots so he rejected montage based upon the notion of continuity in time, space or action. He suggested viewing shots not in an additive way but as exchanges, like lines in poetry. This comprehension of montage emphasized rhythm and the correlating and differentiation underlying artistic abstraction. Such 'jumpy' montage shifts the naturalist-oriented movement within the shot to an abstract rhythmical context and allows the forming of metaphors and symbols. 'Instead of people kissing, we see a pair of turtledoves. Here too the visible thing is fragmented: different performers, different things are presented as semantic equivalents; but at the same time the action itself is split in two, the second part of the equation (turtledoves) giving it its specific semantic coloration.'[37]

Film's artistic merit was to be found in styles and genres that derived from the medium's specific and unique devices of cinematogenicity and montage. He rejected films based on styles and genres borrowed from other art forms, since these were based on these other arts' own specific devices. Hence, for example, he rejected the literary genre of the historical novel. This genre, which mingles historical and fictional figures and facts within a narrative framework, is plausible in literature due to its basic material of words, which do not raise in the reader the question of whether the character resembles the historical figure represented. Hence, the *word* Napoleon does not lead the reader to ask if the character resembles the historical figure. In film, however, the photographed actor immediately raises in the viewer the question of resemblance, undermining the basis that allows this genre to be plausible in literature. In film, whose basic material is photographs, these historical dramas turn into '*a moving portrait gallery*'.[38] This is perhaps why we often sense shallowness, nostalgia and an overall artificiality in historical fictional films, particularly those centred upon historical figures whose image is known to us, such as Hitler, Stalin or Lincoln.[39]

Tynjanov suggested that true genres are only those deriving from the medium's specificity, since 'the question of genre is linked to the question of specific material – and style.'[40]

On the basis of such premises, Tynjanov as well as other Russian formalists valued the 1920s' films of revolutionary Marxists such as Eisenstein, Vertov and Pudovkin, since their 'lyrical' and 'dramatic' films were based on the exaltation of cinematic devices and montage.

2.2 MARXIST CRITIQUES OF FORMALISM

The main opposition to film formalism came from the same revolutionary Marxists whose films the formalists lauded. As mentioned, Vertov rejected altogether the notion of film as art and perceived his cinematic manipulations of documentary shots as a search for truth 'in' the world rather than as detached formalist abstractions. Eisenstein also revealed his aversion to formalism when he criticized Vertov's cinematic manipulations as 'formalist Jackstraws and unmotivated camera mischief', meaning that his manipulations of manifest formal appearances led to misleading formalist abstractions rather than to an understanding of real world processes.[41] As will be seen in Chapter 3, Marxism's major attack on formalism in general and film formalism in particular was based upon the formalist premise that art is an autonomous, abstract striving activity and therefore independent from what Marxists perceived as art's necessary and determining sociopolitical context. In 1927, when *Poetica Kino* was published, Russian formalism was already coming under heavy attack from Soviet quarters, a mounting attack initiated already in 1923 by Leon Trotsky. The movement was finally dispersed and dissolved after Stalin's rise to power and the official adoption of socialist realism as the party's cultural policy.

Roman Jakobson is credited with bringing formalism to the West through his work within the Prague Linguistic Circle, whose ideas influenced American and West European poetic studies. In any case, formalism resurfaced in the West during the 1960s. Noel Burch, its main proponent in film, developed somewhat paradoxically a neo-formalist approach based on the originally Marxist concept of the dialectic (devoid of Marxist materialist ideology) to articulate a meticulous theory of film based on a typology of sound/image, space/time and off/on screen relations. Burch argued that dialectical or rather asymmetrical or contradictory intra- and interrelations drew attention to cinematic formal qualities and enhanced the abstracting power of film as art. However, influenced by the period's flowering neo-Marxism, Burch critiqued in retrospect 'the source of embarrassment' of his early work as 'Formalism. A formalism of the worst kind ... *flight from meaning* ... a neurotic rejection of "content" [which] stemmed from a studied ignorance, and *fear* of the political.'[42] Hence, for Marxists and neo-Marxists alike, with the notable exception of the Frankfurt School,[43] formalism was anti-revolutionary and embedded capitalist ideology or even supported fascist politics. As succinctly put by Walter Benjamin, '"*Fiat ars – pereat mundus*" says Fascism... This is evidently the consummation of "*l'art pour l'art*" [i.e. formalism] ... This is the situation of politics which Fascism is rendering aesthetic. Communism responds by politicizing art.'[44]

3 FILM AS SIMULACRUM

While Marxists of the 1920s and neo-Marxists of the 1960s critiqued film formalism for abstracting reality and film realism for mystifying it, they shared with the formalists the presumption that reality is out there and that films react to it. This long held presumption came under attack with the advent of the postmodern episteme in the 1970s. Postmodernists suggested that 'reality', if existent at all is always-already present in people's mind as textual fabrication. Moreover, if there is something termed reality, it is preceded by models or simulations that actually generate whatever is defined by them as 'reality'. As Baudrillard described it, 'the empirical object, to which qualities of shape, colour, matter, function and discourse are assigned ... is a myth ... it is nothing but the types of relations and different meanings converging and swirling around it'.[45]

This postmodern perception gradually invaded different disciplines. Hence, historian Hayden White rejected the historian's pretension to reveal humanity's past through historical facts. Facts are in his view nothing more than texts that mediate an always-already mediated reality. The historian, rather than dealing with facts in an attempt to reveal an elusive past, constructs this past to begin with according to the structuring possibilities allowed by language or other communicative systems such as film.[46] A similar revolution occurred in the conception of scientific research when the philosopher of science Thomas Kuhn argued that scientists are driven in their research by a set of conventions and institutional directives.[47] Contrary to positions on scientific research such as that of Karl Popper (whose ideal was the search for truth through constant attempts at refuting scientific hypotheses, claiming that the more a hypotheses poses conditions that may lead to its refutation the more scientific it is), Kuhn contended that the evolution of scientific research is characterized by the upholding of theories until there is so much contradicting data that it becomes impossible to cling on to them. Moreover, claimed Kuhn, there is no assurance whatsoever that the new theory is any better than the one it replaced. The radical questioning of our ability to know the world was further complicated by Michel Foucault's position that the search for truth is in itself nothing more than a powerful discourse competing with other discourses within the cultural configurations of power. There is not one truth claimed Foucault, only discursive truisms.

For Baudrillard in particular there seemed to be no 'external' reality or truth at all. Hence, argued Baudrillard, it is not the case that somewhere beyond our faculties there is a reality mediated to us by images, but rather that reality *is* an image, that it is nothing but simulacrum. In 'Simulacra and Simulations'[48] he argued that the simulacrum, which was always present yet obscured, gradually came to the fore. Whereas earlier the image was discussed in terms of its reproducing or distorting a reality that presumably preceded it, today it seemed clear that all those early pre-suppositions were untenable mental manipulations aimed at safeguarding the fact that reality does not exist, thereby constituting fake hierarchies among different types of simulations. He found evidence for this in his interpretation of iconoclasm (the action of destroying sacred images) as an act aimed at preventing the revelation that there is nothing that the image embeds. He went on to find in different disciplines strategies aimed at safeguarding them from the revelation that what they position as the 'authentic' component legitimizing their quest is an empty simulacrum. Hence, in citing Molière's *The Imaginary Invalid* he showed how Argan's illness is described as imaginary based on the presumption that there are 'real' illnesses. However, asked Baudrillard, how about the hypochondriac who actually develops physical symptoms? In what sense is his simulation different from the medical simulations termed 'real'? Likewise, he ridiculed a French military court questionnaire designed to detect whether a soldier is feigning a mental illness, in its implication that anyone answering the questionnaire's simulation 'correctly' is 'really' mentally disturbed and should be exempted from duty. Also, he recounted how a simulated replica of an ancient tomb was placed near the 'real' one for tourists to visit, an action aimed at safeguarding the fake authority of the ancient simulation as origin. In discussing Disneyland, Baudrillard wrote that 'Disneyland is presented as imaginary in order to make us believe that the rest is real, when in fact all of Los Angeles and the America surrounding it are no longer real, but of the order of the hyperreal and of simulation … the real is no longer real.'[49] Finally, in a curious book entitled *The Gulf War Never Happened* (1995), Baudrillard questioned the actual occurrence of the first Gulf war. Claiming that all of our knowledge on this war came from CNN reports showing Tomahawk missiles being launched, explanations offered by General Schwartzkopf on the proceeding of the war, and the use of computerized simulations, Baudrillard suggested that the war was nothing but simulation.

Notwithstanding the far-fetched nature of some of Baudrillard's claims, his notion of simulacrum informs many contemporary films. *Wag the Dog* (1998), for instance, recalls Baudrillard in its dealing with a simulated TV war aimed at rescuing the American president from a sex scandal before elections. In a key scene, a Hollywood producer recruited to generate this political spin (Dustin Hoffman) takes a photograph in his studio of a wretchedly dressed girl and digitally places her in the midst of the ruins of a bombarded town in order to evoke the sympathies of the American people for the poor 'Albanian refugee'. *The Matrix* (1999), telling the story of a computer hacker who learns from mysterious rebels that reality is only a huge simulation, explicitly references Baudrillard when the film's protagonist Neo (Keanu Reeves) is seen with a copy of Baudrillard's 'Simulacra and Simulation'. The far-fetchedness of the film's idea that the reality experienced by humans is nothing but a simulation programmed by machines who suck through this simulation the human energy they need to keep their underworld going implies that neither world nor underworld is more than a simulation. The film's stunning digital effects make tangible the idea of reality-as-simulation through Neo's gradual empowerment to

Documentary Filmmaking: From the Photogenic to the Simulacrum

The belief in the power of cinematographic reproduction and editing to reveal hidden aspects of reality was the cardinal rationale for modernist documentary filmmaking, both by filmmakers sharing this belief, and by those who manipulated it for ideological and even propagandistic purposes. Whatever the aims driving them, their cinematography and editing always involved a conscious and subjective manipulation given the necessity of selection and narrative deployment. Vertov's awareness of this led him to include within his films the process of the film's production in its relation to the resulting images and their editing. In his film *Man with a Movie Camera* (1929), Vertov constantly shows himself, the camera, his cameramen and editor as they work on the gathering and editing of shots, emphasizing the direct relation between the shooting and the shot, the editing and the edited. In

an emblematic sequence within the film, his editor and wife Svilova is shown working by the editing table as she tries to match a shot of a child smiling with that of an elderly woman, shifting back and forth from the matching process to the matched result. Each result is different rhythmically and thematically so that one match emphasizes the difference in age while another focuses on the similarity of the smile. This comes through not only because of the shifting interrelations but also from their relation to shots showing Svilova in the process of interrelating them, as when Svilova is shown at the editing table setting a freeze-frame of the girl in motion and exposing her bursting smile. In sharp contrast to Vertov's self-reflexivity and awareness stands Robert Flaherty's manipulative style as found in his poetic documentary *Nanook of the North*. In the film, Flaherty used the viewer's belief in documentary

manipulate it by floating within it or by slowing, accelerating or elasticizing it. This relation between the digital revolution and Baudrillard's concept of the simulacrum has often been noticed by researchers. Hence, Vivian Sobchack has suggested that the digital device of morphing instantiates Baudrillard's simulacrum in that the morph has no origin whatsoever, since that from which it changes does not 'cause' or precede that to which it has changed. The morph implies seamless reversibility and one image is not more real, original or essentially different from the other. For instance, she recapitulates Baudrillard's ideas in a comparison she makes between the pre-morph film transformations in a montage sequence from *All that Jazz* (1979), showing a mix of ethnic and gender differentiated dancers' bodies constituting one single pirouette, to Michael Jackson's morphing of similar bodies into one another in his *Black or White* videoclip (1991). She argues that whereas through cut transitions in *All that Jazz*, 'we are still aware of their discretion and diference ... in *Black or White* ... these racially and ethnically "different" singing heads enjoy no discretion:

---

images to depict an anachronistic, embellished, exotic and faked image of Eskimo life. He did this by re-creating through the leading Eskimo character Nanook, the way Eskimos used to dress and hunt in the past, a task which Nanook had no knowledge of and had to learn and perform at great risk. The manipulation of documentary images was also exploited for purely propagandistic purposes in many state-subsidized films and reached extremely troublesome proportions as in the Nazi film *The Eternal Jew* (1940), where Jews are equated with dirty and disgustingly presented rats by the juxtaposition of unflattering documentary images of Jews with those of rats.

Aware of the problematic subjective import embedded in documentary shots and editing yet still believing in the medium's power to reveal some truth, two main and contradictory strains of documentary

filmmaking developed during the 1960s. In the USA, Robert Drew and others initiated the *Direct Cinema* movement characterizing it as a 'fly on the wall' attitude towards the reality recorded. They used several hand-held cameras to cover an event, imparting a sense of liveliness and non-intervention as evident in their multi-camera coverage of the 1960 Democratic Convention (*Primary*, 1960). In contrast, the French anthropologist Jean Rouch initiated what he termed a *cinéma verité* movement (a term borrowed from Vertov's newsreel series *Kino-Pravda/Film Truth*), in which the filmmaker made himself and his subjectivity present throughout the film, going beyond Vertov's manifestation of the filmmaking process by the constant interrogation of the premises guiding the coverage of events. This can be seen in Rouch's film *Chronicle of a Summer* (1961) where, towards the end, those interviewed in

each is never "itself" but rather a mutable permutation of a single self-similarity [as Jean Baudrillard writes] "Division has been replaced by mere propagation".[50]

The idea that morphing is based on the propagation of inter-referring simulations that deny meaningful categorical or hierarchical differentiations pervades many contemporary films. This can be found in the widespread device of digital replication and multiplication of the same character (e.g. Mr Smith the virus agent in *The Matrix*), but is also evident in the destabilization of real versus fictional characters or environments in films. Well-known cases include Ridley Scott's director's cut version

the film as well as the director conduct a discussion over the truth import and manipulations of the film just shown. This latter strain has developed into first-person documentaries as found in David Perlov's six-part film *Diary* (1973–83), where the pretension to reveal objective truth is discarded to begin with in favour of a documentation of the director's immediate surroundings as seen through his hand-held camera. Through his own voice-over commentary, his preferred music and paintings, the director portrays a highly subjective and poeticized view of his world.

The advent of the postmodern episteme and the dominant concept of the simulacrum blurred the distinction between fact and fiction. Postmodernists rejected the assumption maintained by both documentary realists and formalists that reality exists beyond human perception and can be revealed (realists) or must be departed from (formalists). Postmodern filmmakers presumed from the outset that while documentary and fiction are cultural categories or kinds of discourse with different styling, their distinction does not stem from their approach to an elusive pre-recorded reality. Hence, postmodern films inadvertently and seamlessly mixed documentary and fiction. Deliberate documentary-style lies and fictional truisms abounded. For example, in Israeli filmmaker Avi Mugrabi's film *How I Learned to Overcome my Fear and Love Arik Sharon* (1997) the director mixes a documentary following of Ariel Sharon's election campaign with a deceitful documentation of both his slow transformation into one of Sharon's devotees and the deterioration of his marital relations, ending with his wife's decision to leave him because of his changed

of *Blade Runner* (1982) – where Deckard, a 'blade runner' in charge of tracking down and terminating replicants turns out to be a replicant himself – and David Cronenberg's film *eXistenZ* (1999) – where a game designer creates a virtual-reality game that taps into the players' body and mind but ultimately leaves them (and us) with the idea that the 'reality' from which the film started may have been just another option within the game. Other film researchers following Baudrillard's notion of simulacrum have noticed that contemporary films are leaning towards stunning spectacles on account of narrative or character depth.

political affiliation. Woody Allen's *Zelig* (1983) offers a good illustration of the blurred postmodern distinction between fact and fiction. The film is articulated in various documentary styles such as the use of voice-over commentary over jumpy edited segments of grainy or scratched 'old-looking' black and white archival film footage, inserted within modern-looking interviews in colour. Through this style the film tells the story of Zelig, a human chameleon who adapts his looks and personality to whatever period, place or circumstances he finds himself in. Moreover, Zelig is seamlessly inserted into famous documentary photographs and film clips, as when he is seen sitting among the Nazi leadership near Hitler. Instantiating postmodern approaches to film, *Zelig*, comically blurs in both style and content the categorical distinctions between documentary and fiction, film and reality, different historical periods and different identities. Postmodernism has also led to what have been called *mocumentaries*, such as the *Blair Witch Project* (1999) which opens with a caption reading 'In October of 1994, three student filmmakers disappeared in the woods of Burkittsville, Maryland, while shooting a documentary. A year later their footage was found.' The film uses hand-held cameras offering an unnoticed mix of fact, fiction and deliberate documentary styled lies to fabricate its fictional mystery. The latest manipulation of reality can be seen in the widespread 'Reality TV' genre (e.g. *Big Brother*) where ordinary people are under surveillance by cameras recording their intimate life while competing for some prize.

Chapter Summary

- For realists, the photogenic implies the cine-camera's unique ability to *reveal* hidden dimensions of the photographed object.
- For formalists, the photogenic is an aesthetic quality derived solely from film's stylistic *transformations and abstractions* of the recorded images.
- Baudrillard's postmodern concept of the simulacrum implies that film is neither a reproduction of reality nor its formalist abstraction since reality itself is a simulation.

Realists

- For Jean Epstein, the photogenic in film evokes in the viewing subject a *lyrosophical* unmediated emotional knowledge of the world by addressing the visual sense through images in motion.
- Dziga Vertov's Marxist notion of *film-truth* called for the exclusive use of documentary shots to decipher society's class structure.
- André Bazin claimed that film's calling was to reveal the world's beauty through long deep-focused shots and the minimal use of editing.
- Neo-Marxists and psychoanalysts critiqued film realism on the grounds that film representations of 'reality' impart the notion that reality's essence is spiritual.
- Cognitivists rejected the realist presumption that film causes viewers to believe in the reality represented since viewers are aware that the film is a reproduction.

Formalists

- Tynjanov argued that any object can become photogenic since the photogenic is a result of stylistic transformations.
- For the formalists the two main devices specific to film were the cinematogenic (the stylistic transformation of objects due to the camera's 'distortions') and the montage (the 'mounting' or editing of film shots).
- Marxists attacked the formalist premise that film as art is autonomous and independent from its determining sociopolitical context.

Postmodernists

- For Baudrillard, humans inhabit a virtual or hyper reality since reality *is* an image. *The Matrix* offered stunning digital effects that made tangible the idea of reality-as-simulation.
- Postmodernist film documentarists suggest that documentary and fiction are simply different kinds of simulations and seamlessly mix documentary and fiction.

2 FILM CONSTRUCTS

INTRODUCTION

Semiological and structural approaches that developed in the 1950s strove to decipher some deep underlying sign system (semiology) or structure (structuralism) able to explain or reveal the meaning of a variety of surface features. Their methods were used by film analysts to explain how films communicate meaning or the affinities between films subsumed under the categories of author, genre and narrative. Influenced by the formalist school[1] and based upon the structural linguistics developed by Ferdinand de Saussure[2] and published in 1916, they began to analyse the specific sign system underlying cinema and the specific meaning conveyed by the deep structure of groups of films. This was done according to repetitions and variations of specific constitutive elements. Particularly productive was the semiological analysis of classical cinema's editing system and the structural analysis of films belonging to the western film genre.

From the 1970s poststructuralists began questioning the grounds upon which semiologists or structuralists grouped films, along with their notion of deep structures, offering instead the ideas of intertextuality, constant flux and polysemy (i.e. the presumption that a film conveys different simultaneous meanings rather than one 'true' meaning). Their approach was based upon the conception of film-system, film genre, auteur or narrative as open ended, not necessarily cohering processes, *interacting* with subjective and identity-shifting spectators that offer different and multiple *readings*. They considered their approach to be a correction to what they perceived as a futile search on the part of semiologists and structuralists for fixed systems and groupings embedding fixed meanings.

Film cognitivists on the other hand, while also turning their attention during the 1980s to how spectators interact with films, did not forgo the films' or the spectators' striving for coherence. They offered instead aware viewers, actively engaged in the cognitive construction of a film whose various formal devices playfully puzzle or satisfy the spectators' striving for coherence. In what follows we will trace this shifting conception of film constructs.

1 SAUSSURE, SEMIOLOGY, STRUCTURALISM AND FILM CONSTRUCTS

1.1 FERDINAND DE SAUSSURE'S KEY LINGUISTIC CONCEPTS

1.1.1 The Arbitrary Nature of Signs in Language.   Based on the fact that in different languages the same object is signalled through different sounds, Saussure reached the conclusion that there is no natural connection between signs or *words* in language and the object or referent outside language that they stand for, that the meaning of a given word derives from the structure of the *language* to which it belongs and not from its relation to whatever it references outside it. Hence, the word 'chair' has nothing in it that resembles a real chair. Even onomatopoeic words, which seem to maintain some kind of sound resemblance to the sound produced by the object they reference, did not shake his conclusion, since different languages offer different onomatopoeic sounds to the same referent. Hence, in the English language a dog's bark is *rough* whereas in Hebrew its *hav*, while the word *bottle* is *bakbuk* in Hebrew. This led Saussure to describe the relation of spoken or written language signs to their referents as *arbitrary*.

Saussure went on to distinguish *within* the sign between the *signifier* (i.e. the material graphic tracing or sound) and the *signified* (i.e. that which comes to mind when we read or hear the signifier). Hence, Saussure differentiated between a sign's referent (e.g. this or that material chair in a given time and place) and its signified (e.g. the mental representation of 'chair'), concluding that while the signified, being in a necessary relation to the signifier, forms part of language, the object referenced by the sign is extraneous to language. From the point of view of language, maintained Saussure, the referent is of no consequence. Within language, however, the relation between the representation of the object in our mind (the signified) and the way it is written or sounds (the signifier) is also arbitrary. There is no resemblance between the representation that comes to our mind when we hear or read the word *chair* and the sequence of letters *c h a i r*. If the letter *c* is deleted, nothing comparable drops from the mental representation of the chair, nor is there any relation or resemblance whatsoever between the signified *chair* and the signified *hair* that results when you omit the *c*. Hence Saussure defined the *sign* in language as an *arbitrary relation between signifier and signified*. He maintained that this arbitrary relation explains the economy of language: by combinations of a small number of signifiers (e.g. letters) we can generate an indefinite number of words and sentences that forge in our minds an indefinite number of signifieds.

Having insulated language signs from the external world, Saussure went on to claim that the value and function of signs in language derives more from their relation to other signs in the language than to something beyond language. This relation is based on a structure of mutual differences between signs, demanding that the sign be *discrete* (enclosed and differentiated) so that its value or function can be defined by its difference from other signs in the language. Hence, the value and function of the letter *A* derives from its difference from all other letters in the alphabet. Saussure applied this structural differential model not only to signifiers but also to their signifieds. Hence, the value and function of the signified *dog* derives from its difference from other signifieds such as *wolf* or *cat*. For instance, cats and wolves do not bark. The structural principle of differences between discrete signs was applied by Saussure to all levels of language (letters, words and sentences). Saussure's favourite example to explain his structural linguistics, according to which the value and function of signs derives from their mutual differences within the system of language, was the game of chess. In chess each piece references an object in the world used in warfare. However, the most experienced general will not gain any knowledge of the game from his war experiences. This is because the value of each piece has nothing to do with what it references in the world and has everything to do with how its movement differs from that of all the other pieces in the game. For example, the diagonal move of the bishop has nothing to do with how bishops move during battle and has everything to do with how its movement differs from the rank-and-file move of the rook or from the knight's L-shaped move.

1.1.2 Language System (Langue) and Speech (Parole). Saussure designed as *language system* (langue) all the rules that determine the possible combinations of signs in language and that allow people to generate comprehensible articulations. He went on to claim that this system, which exists in the minds of all the competent users of a given language, logically precedes any comprehensible *speech* (parole) on their part. From a linguistic point of view, any use of language, whether through writing or speech, is always a concrete realization at a given time and place of the rules of the language system. Without the internalization of the language system in users' minds a communicative use of language is impossible. Moreover, a single individual cannot change the system. I can erase the word *moon* but it will not disappear from the language system. This conception of language implied that it is more accurate to say that a person's world-view is constrained to what his/her language system allows rather than the other way around.

The relation between the language system and its realization in speech or writing is such that the system's existence is prior to any use and it is always synchronous to each realization. The language system's existence, as opposed to its realization, does not depend on a specific time and place of utterance and is therefore reversible in time. Hence, the language system is the *depth structure* of language, while its realization in speech or writing is its *surface manifestation*. Speech or writing on the other hand always follow from the language system, are always uttered at a concrete time and place, and are always diachronic and irreversible (i.e. 'in' the flow of time). For example, from the point of view of the language system, the sentence 'the dog is chasing the cat' has the same meaning today and yesterday. From the point of view of speech, however, the meaning of the sentence shifts according to the time and place of utterance. If I repeat the sentence 'the dog is chasing the cat,' 'the dog is chasing the cat,' each utterance has a different meaning stemming from its unique existence in a certain time and place (e.g. the second time around has a different meaning by the very fact that it is uttered *after* the first time). For Saussure, the science of linguistics can reach scientific conclusions primarily in the study of the language system since the study of speech or writing is fuzzy by definition because it is dependent upon contexts that are extraneous to language (such as who utters the sentence, under what circumstances, or when and where it is uttered).

1.1.3 Paradigm and Syntagm.   Saussure argued that in order to make an utterance in language individuals operate on two axes simultaneously. On the *paradigmatic* axis, or axis of selection, a sign is chosen from the language system internalized in the individual's mind, while on the combinatorial, or *syntagmatic*, axis the chosen sign is combined with another chosen sign. This dual process allows the individual to articulate words and sentences. For example, if I choose the letters *D*, *O* and *G*, I can combine them as *DOG* or as *GOD*. Likewise, in a sentence like 'the dog chased the cat' I can perform a paradigmatic change and choose 'mouse' instead of 'dog', getting 'the mouse chased the cat', or I can perform a syntagmatic change and get 'the cat chased the mouse'. A change on either the paradigmatic or syntagmatic axes changes the meaning of the utterance.

The Saussurean tenet that utterances in language are formed by the axes of selection and combination; his differentiation between the deep structure of language and its surface manifestation in speech; his claim that the meaning, value and functions of language signs derive from their discreteness and from their mutual differences; and his principle of an arbitrary relation between the sign and what it stands for – were premises borrowed by semiologists and structuralists alike in their study of various ways of communication that are not based on written or spoken language.

While some consider Saussurean-derived semiology and structuralism to be identical disciplines,[3] a difference can be traced between the two. Hence, semiologists focus upon the arbitrary *vertical* relation between signifier and signified, searching for the specific language system of ways of communication that are not based on written or spoken language (e.g. film as sign system).[4] Structuralists, on the other hand, overlook this split *within* the sign and focus upon the *horizontal* relations between signs within the structure they constitute (e.g. film genres as structures). As stated by Lévi-Strauss, 'structuralism refuses to set the concrete against the abstract and to recognize a privileged value in the latter. *Form* [e.g. signifiers] is defined by opposition to material other than itself [e.g. signifieds]. But *Structure* has no distinct content; it is content itself, apprehended in a logical organization conceived as a property of the real'.[5]

1.2 SEMIOLOGICAL FILM CONSTRUCTS

Following his study of language, Saussure realized that many of his conclusions might be applicable to sign systems other than linguistic ones. He predicted that linguistics would become a major field within a larger discipline that would also study sign systems not based on written or spoken language. He called this discipline 'semiology', predicting that in non-lingual sign systems, even if their signs are not arbitrary as those of language, the conventional-arbitrary element in them will turn out to be the basis for their meaningful articulation:

> When semiology becomes organized as a science, the question will arise whether or not it properly includes modes of expression based on completely natural signs, such as pantomime. Supposing that the new science welcomes them, its main concern will still be the whole group of systems grounded on the arbitrariness of the sign... Polite formulas, for instance, though often imbued with a certain natural expressiveness (as in the case of a Chinese who greets his emperor by bowing down to the ground nine times), are nonetheless fixed by rule; it is this rule and not the intrinsic value of the gestures that obliges one to use them. Signs that are wholly arbitrary realize better than the others the ideal of the semiological process.[6]

Saussurean-inspired semiologists turned to the study of media such as photography and film whose signs were not arbitrary, realizing that these signs are difficult to isolate because of their non-discrete analogous and continuous nature. This posed a problem given that the deciphering of a code demanded discrete units that could be compared and differentiated from each other. In what follows we will consider two seminal attempts to deal with this problem.

1.2.1 Roland Barthes's Photographic Paradox. The analogous aspect of the photographic sign led Roland Barthes to consider the photographic message a paradox.[7] On the one hand, the photograph appears before our eyes as lacking any code, as an almost direct documentation of whatever stood in front of the camera. On the other hand, the photograph conveys a complex message to the beholder. It is ripe with meaning. Therefore, since according to Barthes's Saussurean premises there cannot be a message without a code, the photograph poses a paradox. Barthes tried to decipher all coded elements within photographs. He noticed that the composition of many photographs has precedents in coded pictorial compositions from a certain period; that some convey meaning through the deployment of discrete elements that form stereotypes (e.g. a person wearing spectacles, smoking a pipe with books in the background signals 'an intellectual'); and that the photograph's angle and distance can be related to a decipherable code (e.g. a low-angled photograph of a person from up close may convey the message that the person is important or threatening). Nevertheless, argued Barthes, despite these codings there always remains a *natural* uncoded element. This element can be fully experienced in what he called *traumatic* photographs (e.g. of mutilated bodies), causing beholders to cut short their chain of signification. Hence, the paradox resurfaces.

This uncoded aspect of photographs subverted Barthes's attempts at codifying them. He then offered an interesting resolution: photographs generate through their uncoded aspects a *naturalization* of meaning. That is, photographs hide their discrete coding in their documentary and analogous look. In this way photographs impart the notion that the message received emanates from the real world. This also explained for Barthes the manipulative persuasive power of photographs. Using Saussure's distinction between signifier and signified, Barthes argued that in the photograph two types of codes coexist in a particular relation to each other. Hence, an analogical, *denotative* code (*pointing* to the world as its signified) in which the signifier cannot be separated from the signified becomes in turn the signifier of a *connotative* discrete code consisting of the meanings evoked in the viewer's mind when looking at discrete portions within the continuous photograph. Barthes characterized this type of articulation as mythical. Myths, he said, are naturalizations of ideologies.[8] He analysed, for instance, the cover of a French magazine figuring a black soldier saluting the French flag. On the one hand, the photograph was analogous, undifferentiated and continuous, conveying something like, 'this is a real event that was documented in which a black soldier was seen saluting the French flag.' On the other hand, discrete elements such as the saluting gesture, the French army uniform, the French flag and the black skin raised in his mind ideological connotations conveying something like, 'Third world people are loyal and respectful to French imperialism.' This ideological connotation seemed to emanate naturally from the photograph's denotation. It was hidden in the photograph and received as a real, factual situation.

1.2.2 Christian Metz's Film as Language System. The idea guiding Christian Metz's semiological analysis of film[9] was that the medium's utterances must have something comparable to a language system that determines the rules of selection and combination of its signs. Metz relied upon Saussure's premise that the arbitrary-conventional aspect of signs is what allows comprehensible utterances even if these signs are not as arbitrary as those of written or spoken language.

Metz began by noting the fact that films mix codes from different language systems. He realized that in this film does not differ from spoken or written language. Like film, the latter also combine their specific language system with other semiological systems such as the system of intonation in speech or of calligraphy in writing. However, while these accompanying semiological systems form part of the meaning imparted by speech or writing, they do not impede the study of language's specific sign system.

This distinction between language systems and their mixed figuration in various texts led Metz, following Saussure's distinction between the language system (langue) and speech (parole), to distinguish between two different types of semiological research: one is concerned with the uncovering of the codes of specific language systems, while the other studies the necessary mix of various semiological systems in their actual manifestation. The realization that manifest film texts are evidently a mixture of several sign systems led him to claim that, if film has its own language system, this system must be specific to the medium and different from any other sign systems found in film texts. Reviewing the sign system of language, he reached the conclusion that beside principles shared by all semiological systems, what primarily differentiates them from each other is the nature of their *signifiers* (e.g. mathematics uses numbers, music uses tones, and written or spoken languages like English, Chinese, Hebrew or Arabic have different signifiers). Moreover, language in general is distinguished from other semiological systems by the nature of its signifiers (i.e. letters), which allow its economy, in that through combinations of a small number of letters an infinite number of words can be formed. Hence Metz concluded that, if film has its own sign system, it can only result from its having unique signifiers whose combinations generate meaningful utterances. Only in such manner can film be considered to have a sign system of its own, independent from other sign systems or their mixture.

In order to decipher film's specific signifiers he turned to study the material base of film, premising that signifiers are 'the matter of expression' as defined by the linguist Hjelmslev. This led him to identify the combination in film of five signifying materials: (1) recorded moving image track; (2) recorded speech; (3) recorded musical track; (4) recorded noise or effects; (5) written material (imprinted captions or subtitles and writing within the image). The combination of these materials allows film to express itself in a unique way that is different from all other semiological systems. For example, the recorded image track can be identically repeated. Likewise, the combination of a recorded music track with a recorded image track allows for sound/image combinations that are impossible in other semiological systems. (In this respect, it should be noted, television and computer-generated sounds and moving images would be semiologically identical to film.)

However, he went on, the semiological complexity of film articulation cannot be coded at this time on the level of the content of the moving images. Differing from Barthes, Metz gave up upon the attempt to decipher arbitrary-conventional aspects within the analogical, continuous and seamlessly moving film sounds and images. While he believed that the analogical moving sound/image film flows are coded, he reached the conclusion that the deciphering of such coding is extremely complex since it must incorporate perceptual, mental and social codes. Hence he concluded that on the level of its sound/image flow, film doesn't seem to have something comparable to written or spoken language's economic 'double articulation' of letters and words (allowing the generation of an indefinite number of words from a small number of letters).[10]

He therefore turned to a level of film articulation that is beyond the audiovisual content, that is, to the level of the *editing* of recorded visuals and sounds. Metz was probably particularly drawn to this level since editing devices such as cuts, dissolves and fades conform to the *unique* and *arbitrary* signifiers so valued by Saussure. Now, thought Metz, if the layout of such signifiers generates in spectators similar signifieds, there is good reason to presume that film has its own sign system (that is, a set of conventional rules on how to order these signifiers). Out of the various signifieds generated by editing constructs, he found one set of signifieds that he could clearly define. This was the set of signifieds having to do with transitions in time and space. It seemed to him that film's arbitrary editing signifiers are arranged in some sort of sign system that allows films to signal a variety of temporal and spatial transitions. Hence, Metz found that films, particularly those pertaining to the classical American cinema (1930–55), offer different recurring editing constructs, each comprised of the same arrangement of signifiers and imparting the same understanding of time/ space relations *irrespective* of the various films' differing visual and aural contents. He called these constructs *syntagms* and proceeded to classify them as follows:[11]

A. *Non-chronological* syntagms:
   A1. *Parallel* syntagms: consist of transitions between unrelated places in different and unrelated times. This type may be said to dominate video-clips for example, where musical rhythm rather than time or space interrelate the various shots.
   A2. *Bracket* syntagms: consist of a transition, within a chronological syntagm, to an autonomous segment consisting of a series of locations in different times. These may be used to convey metaphors as in Eisenstein's

film *October* (1929) where, as he follows General Kerenski's entrance to the Winter Palace, a segment is inserted consisting of shifts back and forth from shots of General Kerenski to shots of a metal peacock, implying that Kerenski is proud as a peacock. The temporal and spatial relations between Kerenski and the peacock are not specified and are irrelevant since the intention is to create a metaphor that is out of time and place.

B. *Chronological* syntagms:

B1. *Descriptive* syntagms: consist of transitions between different shots of the same location that appear simultaneous in time. They often open a film, describing the ambiance and the location where things will happen. Hence many films located in Manhattan open with an aerial long shot of the city, often cut to a closer shot of a street, a fountain may be seen followed by birds taking off, and the window of an apartment where the story begins may conclude the segment.

B2. *Narrative* syntagms: These dominant syntagms branch into linear syntagms and alternate syntagms:

B2.1. *Linear* syntagms: consist of an overall continuity in time and space or of a chronological chain of sequences, each in a different location.

B2.2. *Alternate* syntagms: consist of continuity in time while alternating between two or more locations. This syntagm is often used to create tension and expectation as in D. W. Griffith's scene in *Birth of a Nation* (1915) where settlers besieged by Indians await the arrival of the cavalry. The syntagm alternates between shots of the distressed settlers within a cabin, shots of Indians trying to break in, and shots of the cavalry galloping. This conveys the notion that *while* the settlers are being attacked the cavalry is approaching. Another impressive variation of an alternate syntagm can be seen in Francis Ford Coppola's *Godfather* (1972) where the Mafia head Michael Corleone (played by Al Pacino) is seen in church as his godson is being baptized. Suddenly, as the soundtrack of the music and dialogue within the church continues, the image track starts alternating between five different locations showing the godfather's henchmen as they prepare to execute Corleone's rivals. The spectator understands that *while* Corleone is in church his rivals are being executed simultaneously.

Metz showed that all these syntagms are constructed through specific and recurring combinations of film's unique and arbitrary editing signifiers, and that each time such combination occurs in a film segment the same comprehension of time and space is imparted irrespective of the figured visual or aural contents. Moreover, if a change occurs in the deployment of one of the signifiers, the understanding of the passage of time and space changes or gets confused. He instantiated this by analysing a syntagm that he termed *durative*.[12]

Durative syntagms are constructed as follows: (1) a periodical figuration of a few visual motifs belonging to the same location (e.g. a close up of a hand caressing a face; a lit fireplace; the intertwined legs of a couple; dropping snowflakes seen through a window); (2) use of the same editing transition device throughout the syntagm (e.g. *only* cuts or *only* dissolves); and (3) a consistent sound accompaniment (it can be music, speech, effects or even silence so long as these start with the beginning of the syntagm, consistently accompany it and end when the syntagm is over). As can be seen, all the components defining the syntagm are arbitrary and unique film signifiers. Metz claimed that each time such a combination occurs in a film segment, the comprehension of time and space imparted is that time seems to stand still while the event unfolds. This syntagm does not render the notion that the entire event has developed chronologically (as done by a linear narrative syntagm), but rather that what is shown is a kind of summary of the event. Metz contended that this precise combination is necessary for such a comprehension of time and space, because if the deployment of one of the signifiers is changed (e.g. the visual motifs do not recur; a dissolve is inserted among cuts; the soundtrack changes in the middle), then the understanding of the passage of time and space changes or gets confused. He stated that in all *durative* editing constructs he found the comprehension of the passage of time and space was the same *irrespective* of the content of the images or sounds.

A Durative Syntagm in Kurosawa's *Ran*

A masterfully constructed durative syntagm can be found in Akira Kurosawa's film *Ran* (1985). The syntagm depicts a defeat in battle. Following a linear narrative syntagm comprised of a combination of cinematic signifiers that impart seamless continuity of action, time and space, a durative syntagm starts, signalled by the fading of the realist soundtrack and its replacement by a musical score. The music is accompanied by a series of periodically recurring shots connected through dissolves, showing different agonizingly dying soldiers of the defeated side, interspersed by shots of a descending sun. The syntagm abruptly ends when the sound of a

Given that each syntagm has a stable configuration of arbitrary film signifiers across different films, and that it imparts the same comprehension of temporal and spatial changes irrespective of the audiovisual contents, Metz went on to define a syntagm as a *discrete unit*. He then applied Saussure's principle that the meaning of signs derives from their mutual differences within the sign system, arguing that spectators understand durative syntagms because of their difference from other film-editing syntagms and not because they resemble time/space passages in reality (syntagms are arbitrary in that respect). He therefore reached the conclusion that there exists a paradigm of syntagms internalized in competent filmmakers' and spectators' minds, allowing the former to communicate to the latter film variations in time and space. Such variations were constructed by choosing out of a paradigmatic arsenal a discrete syntagm (e.g. durative) and combining it with another chosen syntagm (e.g. linear), and so on.

In sum, Metz claimed to have unearthed a unique film sign system based on arbitrary and conventional discrete units (syntagms), comprised of recurring combinations of film-specific arbitrary and conventional signifiers (cuts, dissolves, wipes, etc.) through which the medium communicates time/space variations. He based this reconstruction of a portion of the editing sign system of film based upon Saussure's key linguistic concepts – the arbitrary relation between signifier and signified; the distinction between the language system and speech; the paradigmatic and syntagmatic axes of articulation; and the determination of sign values by their mutual difference from other signs.

1.2.3 Peter Wollen's Trichotomic Study of Film. In 'The Semiology of the Cinema'[14] Peter Wollen attempted a correction to faults he found in Saussurean-inspired approaches to film. His major critique concerned the Saussurean exclusive focus upon the arbitrary

---

shot hitting a mounted general from the back is heard, the musical score stops and the film returns to a linear narrative syntagm. This powerful durative syntagm constructs the notion that while time seems to stand still the defeat in battle progresses. It also abstracts the notion of 'tragic defeat' from the specific story told, by its use of music, its correlation of battle shots and a descending sun, and by its *summary* rendition of what went on through the use of recurring visual motifs.[13]

nature of signs and the attendant dismissal of the mimetic aspects abundantly found in semiological systems.[15] He therefore imported into film studies Charles Sanders Peirce's semiotics. Contrary to Saussure's exclusive focus upon the arbitrariness of the sign and its disjunction from its natural referent, Peirce's semiotics focused on different relations signs have to their natural referents.[16]

Hence, in his second trichotomy of signs Peirce divided signs into *indexes, icons* and *symbols*:

- Indexical signs relate to referents according to natural law. Signs such as barometers, sundials, medical symptoms or foot imprints on sand are indexical. The photograph is also indexical since as Peirce described it 'photographs ... are in certain respects exactly like the objects they represent. But this resemblance is due to the photographs having been produced under such circumstances that they were physically forced to correspond point by point to nature.'[17]
- Iconic signs relate to their referents by similarity, as in figurative paintings and in diagrams. The similarity the photograph has to its referent can also be understood as iconic since not all indexical signs resemble their referents (e.g. a barometer does not resemble 'fever').
- Symbols are signs whose relation to their referents is based on arbitrary conventions. Letters, numbers, but also 'the scales of justice or the Christian cross' are symbols.[18] Symbols are the Peircean equivalent of Saussure's arbitrary sign.

Following Peirce, Wollen divided film into a documentary-indexical dimension, an iconic dimension under which he subsumed film's intertextual or inter-artistic references, and a symbolic-conventional dimension. He believed this trichotomy could make up for what he found lacking in Saussurean-inspired semiology and in earlier film theories. Hence, Metz's Saussurean semiology focused on the symbolic dimension on account of the documentary and iconic richness of film, whereas Bazin's realism focused on the indexical aspect of film on account of its rich means of articulation. Also, both Metz and Bazin, he contended, oriented by the dichotomy between nature and culture, discarded the symbolic elements *within* film images. While Bazin saw these as intrusions into natural beauty, Metz considered them to be unstable, poor or borrowed from other media. Thus Metz mentioned that the symbolic conventional opposition of good and bad, through the opposing white and black shirts worn respectively by hero and villain in westerns was discarded very early in the genre.[19] While such examples may be poor, contended Wollen, many complex and stable audiovisual symbolizations in film can be mentioned such as Hitchcock's *The Birds* (and, I might add, the figuration of nature in westerns or the scream and the use of off-screen space in horror films). Bazin and Metz also disregarded film iconography. This dimension, neither symbolic nor indexical, comprised according to Wollen a large part of the medium's means of expression. He mentioned in this respect Von Sternberg's films, which he found 'detached from the indexical in order to conjure up a world, comprehensible by virtue of resemblances to the natural world, yet other than it, a kind of dream world, a heterocosm.'[20] To this iconic dimension Wollen also ascribed animation films as well as the entire arsenal of inter-filmic quotations (Brian de Palma's formal playful quotation in *The Untouchables* [1987] of Eisenstein's 'Odessa steps' sequence from *Battleship Potemkin* [1927] comes to mind). Finally, having unearthed what he considered the poverty of the Saussurean semiological approach to film, Wollen suggested, when mentioning the work of Jean-Luc Godard whose films offered 'conceptual meaning, pictorial beauty and documentary truth',[21] that film should be studied in all its dimensions.

However, while Wollen's critique of the application of Saussurean semiology to film unearthed dimensions left untapped by Metz and others, his own Peircean semiotic approach did not go beyond Metz in explaining how films generate meaning. Wollen lacked any kind of structural or other systematic consideration of iconic and indexical oriented signs that could explain their particular way of conveying meaning. Wollen offered a typology of film dimensions, not a method. This may have been what led him to shift his interest from a search of how films communicate meaning to their aesthetic effects: 'Peirce wanted logic and a rhetoric which would be based on all three aspects. It is only by considering the interaction of the three different dimensions of the cinema that we can understand its aesthetic effect.'[22] How about film's logic and rhetoric then? How is the documentary articulation different from the iconic one in terms of meaning? What type of interrelation exists between these dimensions? Wollen is silent on these questions, as is semiology to this day.

Structuralism, another offshoot of Saussure, offered an approach to the understanding of how films construct meaning based upon the concept of 'gross constituent units,' bypassing both the Saussurean dichotomy within the sign between signifier and signified and Peirce's trichotomy of the sign.

1.3 LÉVI-STRAUSS'S STRUCTURAL METHOD

While structuralism has different methods,[23] I will focus on Lévi-Strauss. This is because his approach, particularly as found in 'The Structural Study of Myth',[24] has influenced film studies.

According to Lévi-Strauss, the method of investigation of any cultural phenomenon begins by the simultaneous delineation of its boundaries and the detection, mostly through statistical recurrence, of the discrete units constituting it. The outlining of the phenomenon's boundaries is determined by its constituent units and vice versa.[25] As in Sassure's study, the value or meaning of these constituent units derives more from their mutual interrelations than from their relation to elements outside the phenomenon's boundaries. This value or meaning can be decoded by the positioning of the constitutive units in *binary oppositions* to each other (i.e. each time two units are placed one against the other, allowing their mutual understanding by noting the similarities and differences between them).[26] The layout of relations between these constituent units unearths the deep structure of the studied phenomenon. That is, it unearths the structure that in turn determines the meaning of the constituent units. There is no use, according to Lévi-Strauss, in studying the connection between two constituent units pertaining to different deep structures just because there is a phenomenological or 'natural' relation between them, since each unit's meaning derives from its interrelation with other units *within* the same structure. For example, in a structural study of kinship in a certain society it may turn out that the authority of the uncle on the mother's side is higher than that of the father, whereas in a different society it is lower. However, this 'natural' based comparison would be useless since a structural study may reveal the uncle's authority in society A to be closer to that of the grandmother in society B, whereas in society B his authority may turn out to be closer to that of the second son in society A.

In 'The Structural Study of Myth' Lévi-Strauss applied this approach to the study of the different versions pertaining to the same myth. He likened previous attempts to interpret myths as representing events in society or general emotions to the futile attempts made by linguists before Saussure to find a relation between the sounding of a word and the object it references. Hence, if a myth figured an evil grandmother these researchers claimed that the society where such myth was told considered grandmothers to be evil. However, if grandmothers were not found to be evil in society then researchers claimed that the myth represented repressed feelings towards grandmothers. He claimed that, since myth is part of language in that it is a written or told story, the structural linguistic method developed by Saussure has to be applied: 'everybody will agree that the Saussurean principle of the arbitrary character of linguistic signs was a prerequisite for the accession of linguistics to the scientific level.'[27] Hence, argued Lévi-Strauss, myth has to be considered as being constituted by discrete units. Its meaning does not stem from the natural or objective meaning of each or all units, but from the way these units are interrelated. Moreover, Lévi-Strauss tried to apply to the study of myth Saussure's distinction between the synchronic aspects of language systems (whose components exist simultaneously in the language users' minds and are not ordered in time sequences) and the use of the system as it is manifested in speech, a use which is always diachronic (i.e. always within an irreversible time sequence). Accordingly, he suggested the unearthing of a presumed deep synchronic structure in myths out of its manifestation in the many diachronic versions of mythical stories.[28] He argued that myths intimate this approach. Hence, he noticed that mythical stories are characterized, on the one hand, by their telling a unique story belonging to a society's past, while, on the other, it appears as though these stories can happen any time. Moreover, myths describe unique events that often appear without narrative, temporal, spatial or character motivation and yet there is a feeling that all myths are alike.

In order to instantiate his method Lévi-Strauss chose to study the different versions of the Oedipus myth. While the results of his analysis are questionable, it does offer a good example of his method.[29]

In studying the various versions of the myth, Lévi-Strauss found that the same types of relations distinctly recur within and across the various versions, without any logical relation to the story succession. Hence he reached the conclusion that the myth wants to draw attention to its deep structure rather than to its developing story. He defined these types of relations recurring in the myth's story as the myth's constituent units. Claiming that story is a level of language that is higher than sentences, words and letters and yet manifests the same relational structure pertaining to these lower levels, he decided to call these story units 'mythemes' in their being 'gross' constituent units of language, that is, units of a higher order than phonemes or monemes, yet manifesting the same relational structure.[30] He then suggested a rearrangement of the myth in such a way that each recurring type of relation is grouped together and yet the evolving story order of the myth is maintained.

Hence, if the story line proceeds along the following numbers (each representing a relation in the story): 1, 2, 4, 3, 2, 4, 1, 1, 3, 2, 4, the rearrangement would render the following layout:

```
    1         2
                        4
                   3
              2         4
    1
    1              3
              2         4
```

In such a rearrangement the different types of relations are grouped together in each column but, if you read from left to right and from top to bottom, the story line is maintained. Thus a synchronic reading of the myth (i.e. by columns) is superimposed upon its diachronically evolving story line.

Following this rearrangement of the Oedipus myth, Lévi-Strauss found the following four types of similar relations: (1) sexual attraction between family relatives (a brother desires a sister; a son desires his mother); (2) hostile relations between family relatives (brothers kill each other; a son murders his father); (3) the idea that humans are born from the earth is rejected (a strange conclusion reached by Lévi-Strauss from the myth's figuration of monsters that have to be killed for humans to be born from the earth, implying that humans may originate from different sources); (4) the idea that humans are born from the earth is embraced (a conclusion reached from the grouping of the similar meaning of names of heroes that denote some type of deformation of the leg, believed by ancient Greeks to indicate birth from the earth).

Having grouped the recurring types of relations into constituent units, Lévi-Strauss proceeded to position them in binary oppositions so as to unearth the myth's deep synchronic structure. This revealed that the first two columns offer contradictory views on family relations, while the last two columns offer contradictory views on the idea that humans originate from the earth. He then positioned columns 1 and 2 in binary opposition to columns 3 and 4 based on the issue shared by all columns, which he found to be 'the origin of humans'. Hence, while columns 1 and 2 reject and embrace the idea that humans originate from other humans, columns 3 and 4 reject and embrace the idea that humans originate from the earth. Having gone this far, Lévi-Strauss now noticed that columns 1 and 2 refer to the Greeks' life experiences, whereas columns 3 and 4 refer to their 'cosmology' or religion. Therefore he reached the conclusion that the main contradiction expressed by the Oedipus myth is between the ancient Greeks' life experiences (humans are born from humans) and their religion (humans are born from the earth). He then noticed that what the myth does is to offer a kind of solution to this irresolvable contradiction, which probably bothered the ancient Greeks very much. Hence he maintained that the myth 'resolves' this contradiction between life and religion by turning the contradiction between columns 1 and 2 (life experience) and columns 3 and 4 (religion) into an equivalence 'by the assertion that contradictory relationships [i.e. between life experiences and religion] are identical inasmuch as they are both self-contradictory in a similar way'. Hence, he claimed, since in life as in religion there are contradicting evidences as to the origin of humans, 'social life validates cosmology by its similarity of structure [i.e. similar contradiction]'.[31]

Lévi-Strauss proceeded to find variations upon this logical procedure in different myths pertaining to different cultures.[32] He concluded that the function of myth is to offer a fictive solution to irresolvable contradictions on issues that are extremely important to the society entertaining the myth. The fact that the contradiction is irresolvable and bothering explained in his view why new versions of myths offering fictive solutions keep coming out. It also explained why myths seem similar to each other across cultures. This was because myths are 'mythical' because of their shared peculiar deep structure and not because of the specific and concrete events they tell us about.

1.4 STRUCTURAL FILM CONSTRUCTS

Lévi-Strauss's structural method, particularly his structural study of myth, served as the basis for structural analyses of groups of films evidencing similar characteristics, among other reasons because films were perceived as the myths of modern secular societies, attempting to resolve their bothering contradictions. As stated by Thomas Schatz, 'the genre film represents a distinct manifestation of contemporary society's basic mythic impulse, its desire to confront elemental conflicts inherent in modern culture'.[33] Lévi-Strauss's method offered a way to map the film's recurring elements and generate feasible explanations of the films. Film genres, the films of prominent directors and films exhibiting similar narratives were considered by structuralists to be types of mythical articulations.

What is common to all structural film analyses is their grouping of films under the categories of genre, author or narrative according to their recurring elements; the reduction of such elements to a common denominator that reveals the films' constitutive units; and the binary analysis of these units' interrelations so as to decode the central contradictions dealt with by these films in their deep structure.

1.4.1 Structural Genre Constructs – the Western. While structuralists studied different film genres, the Lévi-Straussean structural analysis of the western stands out because of its characteristic recurrence of iconographic, narrative and thematic motifs. According to Lévi-Strauss, analysis should start with an identification of the genre's constituent units. Here are some of the western genre's classic and most characteristic recurring constituent units ordered in such manner that already intimates their binary oppositions:

Major characters and their visual representation:

- The protagonist: usually a male arriving from nature into town and returning to nature at the end of the film (e.g. *Shane*, 1953); his attire combines Indian and cowboy motifs; highly competent in riding horses and in the use of guns; stronger than all those around him, independent, true to himself and while having committed some crime in the past he is honest, just and good; shot from below to enhance his authority and in non-balanced compositions or irregular camera motions that enhance his freedom and mobility.
- The antagonist: usually a male who arrives from nature (or from 'the East') and is killed by the protagonist in a shoot-out; his attire is fancy, with elements from the East coast along with Indian and cowboy motifs; highly competent in riding horses and in the use of guns; stronger than all those around him except the protagonist, independent, true to himself, criminal, evil, dishonest

and motivated by greed; shot from below to enhance his authority and in non-balanced compositions or irregular camera motions that enhance his freedom and mobility.

- The decent female heroine: often a teacher and blonde (e.g. *High Noon*, 1952); dressed in modest clothes; honest and loyal but weak and dependent; in love with the protagonist and morally 'good'; often shot from above or at eye level to emphasize her vulnerability and in balanced compositions and smooth camera motions that enhance her goodness.

- The indecent female heroine: often a bar dancer and black haired; dressed provocatively; independent and disloyal; in love with the protagonist, good hearted 'deep' inside yet morally 'bad'; often shot from above or at eye level to enhance her vulnerability but in non-balanced compositions and irregular camera motions that enhance her freedom and mobility.

- The town's drunk: Usually arrived in town from the 'East' following moral misconduct; his Eastern US attire is worn out; weak and dependent but good hearted; helps the protagonist; shot from above to enhance his weakness and through irregular camera motions and non-balanced compositions that enhance his being an outsider and drunk.

- Townspeople: immobile and confined to the town; modestly dressed; weak in comparison to protagonist, antagonist, cavalry or Indians and are often un-armed; usually shot at eye level and in balanced compositions to enhance their conformity and stability.

- Homesteaders: immobile in their modest cabin or field; dressed in simple work-ing clothes unfit for riding horses; in conflict with both the protagonist and the antagonist but are weaker than both and are often unarmed; honest, hard working and good; usually shot at eye level and in balanced compositions to enhance their conformity and stability.

- Cowboys: mobile in nature; functionally dressed for horse-riding; are in conflict with the homesteaders or the town people; often dishonest; weaker than the protagonist or antagonist but stronger than the townspeople or the homesteaders; usually shot at eye level to enhance their commonality and in irregular camera motions and non-balanced compositions to enhance their mobility.

- Cavalry: mobile in nature, shot when galloping in orderly formation or when enclosed within military posts; wearing uniforms; stronger than everybody except the protagonist; usually shot from afar, at eye level and in mobile but balanced compositions to enhance their conformity.

- Indians: mobile in nature; fancifully dressed with motifs taken from nature (e.g. feathers, leather); stronger than the townspeople or the homesteaders but weaker than the protagonist, the antagonist and the cavalry; usually shot from afar or in close oblique angles to enhance their common barbarity or evilness (though there are also 'good' Indians); and in non-balanced compositions and mobile irregular camera movements to enhance their freedom and mobility.

The audiovisual figuration of the western's major sites:

- The town: an isolated and undeveloped settlement threatened by forces coming from the surrounding nature; usually consists of one main street; shot overall in balanced compositions.
- Good, benevolent nature: huge open spaces, canyons, rivers or mountain chains; shot overall in balanced compositions to enhance the harmony of man and nature.
- Bad, arid nature: deserts populated by scorpions and snakes; shot overall in non-balanced compositions to enhance danger.
- The bar: a lively and messy place where people drink and smoke; a place frequented by the indecent female heroine, cowboys, the protagonist, the antagonist and the townspeople; shot in non-balanced compositions to enhance disorder.
- The church: a place where the townspeople or homesteaders gather to pray, but also to discuss urgent matters common to the community; shot overall in balanced compositions to enhance conformity.

Horses:

- The protagonist's and the antagonist's horses: loyal, highly trained and efficient; differing in their uniform black or white colour; shot in non-balanced compositions or irregular camera motions that enhance their manoeuvrability.
- The cowboys' horses: loyal, brownish; shot in non-balanced compositions or irregular camera motions that enhance their mobility.
- The Indians' horses: unsaddled 'wild' horses, often mustangs; shot in non-balanced compositions or irregular camera motions that enhance their wildness.
- Townspeople's or homesteaders' horses: heavy and slow moving, often brown carriage-horses; shot in balanced compositions that enhance their commonality.

Firearms:

- Protagonist and antagonist: usually specially decorated pistols.
- Cowboys: functional-looking pistols and rifles.
- Homesteaders: clumsy-looking large rifles.
- Cavalry: functional-looking pistols and rifles, but also swords.
- Indians: Bows and arrows, or feather-decorated rifles.

Having enumerated the genre's constituent units, a process of reduction to major binary oppositions ensues. In brief, most structuralist researchers tend to agree that one of the major binary oppositions and conflicts articulated by westerns and subsuming most of the films' constituent units is that between nature and civilization, considered an endemic irresolvable conflict of American society.[34] This can be seen in the following binary opposition chart where the dominant components of each unit are relegated to one or other column, while *some* of their possible oppositions *within* each column and *between* the columns are mentioned:

	Civilization	vs	Nature
1	Townspeople/homesteaders vs	Protagonist	
2		Protagonist vs	Antagonist
3		Protagonist vs	Indians
4			Good vs bad Indians
5	Cavalry	vs	Indians
6	Decent vs indecent female heroines		
7	Townspeople vs drunk		
8	Town/settlement	vs	Arid nature
9			Benevolent vs arid nature
10	Church vs bar		
11	Settlers' horses and arms	vs	Cowboys' horses and arms
12	Cowboys' horses and arms	vs	Indians' horses and arms
13	Balanced compositions	vs	Non-balanced compositions
14	Smooth camera movement	vs	Shaky camera movement

Discussion of chart: As can be seen the protagonist has been charted as being in-between nature and civilization since he embodies elements taken from both and moves between them. The protagonist carries the genre's contradiction within himself: mobile but longs to settle down; his attire includes cowboy and Indian elements; he fights Indians and the antagonist because he has the ability to fight in nature like they do, but he fights them to save the townspeople or homesteaders. On the deep structural level the conflict is negotiated through the protagonist's pendulum swing between both poles. Hence, he apparently solves the conflict, since through his help nature and its representatives are subdued; but the conflict is reopened, since the protagonist himself usually returns to nature when his work is done. The protagonist is what Lévi-Strauss called a 'trickster' in that he offers a fictive solution to the conflict, by equalizing it within himself.[35] However, equalization is also achieved through the same mechanism that Lévi-Strauss detected in the Oedipus myth. Hence, while there are contradictions between threatening 'bad and arid' nature and threatened civilization (number 8 in chart), there are also contradictions of the same type within nature (such as that between 'good' and 'bad' Indians (number 4)) and within civilization (such as that between the good decent female and the morally bad and indecent one (number 6)). Therefore, it may be concluded that there is no evident conflict between nature and civilization, since within each there are similar moral contradictions and hence nature and civilization are alike. Since this resolution is fictive, following Lévi-Strauss it can be said that as long as the irresolvable conflict between nature and civilization bothers Americans, more versions of the genre will be made.

The binary oppositions between constitutive units generate complex structures as well as different versions and groupings. This is because the value of a constituent unit changes if the opposing unit changes. Hence the unit 'Cowboys' horses and arms' figures under nature when opposed to 'Settlers' horses and arms' (number 11), but is charted under civilization when opposed to 'Indians' horses and arms' (number 12).

However, there may be other columns and conflicts, such as 'order' vs 'chaos,' 'good' vs 'bad' or 'individualism' vs 'collectivism', that may predominate in a western and allow for value changes and even value reversals of constitutive units. Thus, 'law and order' vs 'anarchy and chaos,' usually attributed to civilization and nature respectively, if transposed to determine the conflict between protagonist and townspeople, such as in *High Noon*, may place the protagonist on the side of law and order and the townspeople on the side of anarchy and chaos. Likewise, the binary opposition of 'good' vs 'bad' enhances the fact that some units constituting 'nature' or 'civilization' are 'good' while others are 'bad'. For example, in certain films or periods the unit 'Indians', while remaining under 'nature', changes its value from being 'bad' as in *Stagecoach* (1939) to being 'good' as in *Dances with Wolves* (1991). In the latter film, barbarity is attributed to the cavalry representing civilization, while kindness is attributed to the Indians that represent nature. Finally, overlapping binary oppositions such as 'individualism and good' vs 'collectivism and bad' reveal that units that in some films are constituted 'bad' (e.g. the antagonist) shift their value when placed within such overlapped conflict (the protagonist *and* the antagonist are individualists and hence good), while others that are constituted good (e.g. the homesteaders) shift to bad (the homesteaders *and* the Indians are collectives, hence bad). This complexity allows the analysis of specific films within the genre, as well as tracing the genre's evolution in time.

1.4.2 Structural Author Constructs.   A similar analysis to that of genre was conducted on films subsumed under the category of 'author'. As stated by Geoffrey Nowell-Smith,

> The defining characteristics of an author's work are not necessarily those which are most readily apparent. The purpose of criticism thus becomes to uncover behind the superficial contrasts of subject and treatment a hard core of basic and often recondite motifs. The pattern formed by these motifs ... is what gives an author's work its particular structure, both defining it internally and distinguishing one work from another.[36]

Wollen, for example, in 'The Auteur Theory'[37] structurally overlapped upon the western genre's binary opposition of nature and civilization the work of prominent western film directors like John Ford, Howard Hawks and Budd Boetticher. Through their mutual binary oppositions, he claimed that they offer a diverging approach to their shared unique concern with the contradictory aspects of heroism, since 'For the hero, as an individual, death is an absolute limit which cannot be transcended; it renders the life which preceded it meaningless, absurd. How then can there be any meaningful individual action during life?'[38] Thus, opposing John Ford to Hawks and Boetticher, he reached the conclusion that Ford initially suggested resolving this contradiction by placing the individual within an American society that has 'transcendent values in the historic vocation of America as a nation, to bring civilization to a savage land'.[39] This he found in Ford's early film *My Darling Clementine* (1946) where Wyatt Earp the protagonist offers 'an uncomplicated passage from nature to culture'.[40] However, said Wollen, the hero contradiction is reinstated by Ford in his later films, through a gradual and complex inversion of the values of nature and civilization, so that Ethan Edwards in *the Searchers* (1956) 'unlike Earp, remains a nomad throughout the film'.[41]

1.4.3 Structural Narrative Constructs.   One major problem with the application of Lévi-Strauss's method faced by structuralist film researchers had to do with his neglect of the diachronic narrative dimension of myths. Hence, while Lévi-Strauss bothered to rearrange the myth so that it maintains its plot line *as* it reveals the synchronic columns constituting its deep structure, he ultimately treated the plot's evolution as inconsequential to the myth's equalizing strategies. While he justified this neglect by arguing that such an approach was applicable to ancient myths where the logic of the story seems to be constantly undermined (a claim complicating the application of his method to films), researchers found in Vladimir Propp's *Morphology of the Folktale*[42] an attempt to discern the structural organization of plot development in fairy tales, which are also ancient stories exhibiting an 'incoherence' similar to myths.

Hence, in his study, Propp focused on the *sequence* of events in 100 fairy tales. He found that while the specific content may vary, they all exhibit a striking similarity if we attend to their sequence of 'functions', defined as 'an act of a character, defined from the point of view of its significance for the course of the action.'[43] Propp went on to discern thirty-one functions altogether, which he abridged into single terms such as 'absence', 'interdiction', 'flight', 'violation', 'donor', etc. He found that while some of the functions may be absent in some fairy tales, sometimes because the plot branches into two possibilities, the *sequence* of their appearance remains the same. A very abridged and lacking sequence would develop as follows: an initial situation is established followed by a character going away. This absence leads to some misfortune (through the violation of an interdiction or obedience to an injunction). This misfortune is related to a villain who receives information about his victim and deceives him in order to cause him harm. The hero receives from a donor a gift that carries the hero away to eventually battle the villain. He achieves victory, rescues the victim, returns and gets a reward.[44] Propp noted that while there may be complications or repetitions, the overall sequence of actions remains the same; there are no functions other than the thirty-one he discerned; and their ordering and arrangement 'occurs with logical and aesthetic necessity'.[45] Although Lévi-Strauss properly accused Propp of formalism devoid of context, Propp's structuration of a fairy tale's diachronic development addressed an omission in Lévi-Strauss's synchronic structural method. Film researchers contended that if such structuration occurs in ancient fairy tales, it certainly occurs in film genres, whose constituent units are laid out within a well-thought-out and logically developing narrative.

An interesting attempt to correlate the Lévi-Straussean inspired study of the western genre's deep synchronic structure with a Proppian inspired study of the genre's diachronic plot structure was made by Will Wright in his book *Sixguns and* Society.[46] Contrary to Lévi-Strauss, Wright maintained that while deep structures point to the genre's recurring elements and central contradictions, diachronic narrative structures articulate different resolutions to these contradictions. Furthermore, the study of the diachronic development of films may explain changes in the genre that stem from the different narrative resolutions to the same basic conflicts. Hence, in Wright's view, constituent units change their value not only because of their being positioned in different binary oppositions, as Lévi-Strauss suggests, but also because of changes in the evolution of the story. He gives the example of a simple deep structure consisting of a relation of unanswered love between a *prince* and a poor *girl*. This structure consists of two binary oppositions: male/female and rich/poor. Hence, on the deep structure a change in the binary opposition of the constitutive units may generate a change in their value. Such is the case when male opposes rich and female poor, resulting in a story of unanswered love between a rich *princess* and a poor *boy*.

However, constitutive units may also change their value in accordance with changes in the development of the story and its resolution. Thus, we may have a story in which a prince loves a poor girl, the girl does not answer his love and *the prince kills himself*. However, we may also have a different narrative variation: a poor girl loves a prince, the prince ignores her and *the poor girl kills herself*. While in each case the binary oppositions are the same, the order and resolution change the value of gender and class differences. Wright proceeded to implement his revised structural analysis in a study of westerns. Using a combination of the methods of Lévi-Strauss and Vladimir Propp, he set out to trace the way westerns negotiated through their changing types of narratives and resolutions (e.g. the 'revenge' type narrative) the deep-structured conflict between individual and society throughout the genre's history. In his tracing these changes he showed how the genre evolved from offering resolutions through which the individual ends up marrying, settling down and becoming part of society, to later westerns where the individual ends up detaching himself from society.

1.5 CRITIQUES OF SEMIOLOGY AND STRUCTURALISM

Both semiological and structural methods, along with their resulting constructs, came under fire with the emergence of poststructuralism. The major poststructural critique was aimed at the problematic criteria used to define a sign system's or a structure's boundaries, a problem that also called into question the detection of constituting units. If it is impossible ultimately to legitimize the position of a system's boundaries, how can it be determined which units constitute the system? Which units belong and which do not? On what grounds are units exclusively interrelated to each other if they can actually be related to other units that were excluded from the system? This also brought down the conceptual base sustaining the differentiation between deep and manifest structures, for how can the ultimately arbitrary positing of one set of variables as 'determining' another in some unfounded hierarchy be legitimized?

Also, the static nature of structural and semiological systems ultimately failed to account for the change exhibited in textual production. Likewise, their methods failed to explain how humans improvise and generate focalized articulations, or how textual change and interpretational variability result from the interaction between a text and its readers or spectators.

These latter omissions in structural and semiological approaches were also addressed by the cognitivist strain of thought, whose emergence paralleled the rise of poststructuralism. However, while both poststructuralists and cognitivists shifted their focus away from the study of the text as such to the study of its interaction with readers or spectators, poststructuralists ended up rejecting the objective validity of any decoding of textual constructs. Cognitivists on the other hand, did not forgo the notion that film constructs are indeed *in* the text rather than subjectively imposed, nor that these are usually reconstructed successfully by the minds of coherence-seeking spectators. The poststructural and cognitivist revolutions towards film constructs are the respective concern of our next two sections.

2 POSTSTRUCTURALISM AND FILM CONSTRUCTS

Film researchers influenced by semiology and structuralism considered film in general or groups of films to be a closed autonomic system with clear boundaries and a specific internal structure. This premise was accompanied by the belief that research can decode this internal structure. While the relation between the film and its spectators or authors was considered secondary or irrelevant, they also had presumptions about these 'extraneous' factors, namely that spectator and film author are 'enclosed' autonomic entities with consistent and essential identities. All these presumptions, long pondered upon by philosophy, began to be deconstructed in the 1960s with the emergence of what came to be termed poststructuralism in the 1980s. Poststructuralists[47] deconstructed each of these premises, their legitimacy and methodology, in different fields of culture. The consequence of the poststructural revolution in cultural theory, similar in its logic to consequence of the shift from modernist to postmodernist cultural production, was the turn away from the consideration of film texts as enclosed autonomous structures towards their 'open' interrelation with spectators and authors. They henceforth redefined text, spectator, author and reality as 'open', non-consistent and non-essential entities.

2.1 POSTSTRUCTURAL REDEFINITIONS OF THE CATEGORIES OF AUTHOR, GENRE AND NARRATIVE

Poststructuralists questioned the value and legitimacy of the categories under which films were grouped by structuralists. Hence, asked Michel Foucault,[48] how do you decide which texts are subsumed under an author's body of work? Why the obviousness that his grocery store lists should not be included in his work? Anyway, who is this 'author'? Is it the biological entity it refers to? Is it the structural category constructed a posteriori from a group of works carrying the name? If so, doesn't the same body of work generate different author categories? Moreover, are we speaking of the same entity across time? Is a fiction author (to whom authority over the work is ascribed) similar to a scientific author (where authority is usually denied except in fictional mythologies of scientists)? This series of questions dismantled the validity or legitimacy of the structural category of author. It led Foucault to shift his focus of attention away from questions concerning some elusive essence of an 'author', towards the study of the historically shifting discourses on what an author is; the ideological or practical interests each discourse serves; and the consequences of these discourses for people and for textual studies.

A similar procedure was applied by Jacques Derrida to the structural categories of genre, text and narrative. He reached the conclusion that *genre* and *text* (the latter designating the enclosed entities whose grouping constitutes genre), as well as the category *narrative*, which imposes temporal order on texts, are nothing but fictional constructs and meanings artificially imposed upon an endless chain of signifiers. He considered these signifiers to potentially emanate indefinite interpretative possibilities. The deconstruction of these categories had deep consequences for the structural method because if there is no possibility to define boundaries, there is also no place for talking about the structure's constitutive units, since all units may in principle be related to all other units. This also collapsed the notions of deep and manifest structures since lacking the ability to justify unit groupings, the decision to posit one group as determining another is lost.

The resulting postmodern cultural creation as evident in films such as Quentin Tarantino's *Pulp Fiction* (1994) is characterized by the scrambling of temporal order, the mixing of genres, a pastiche of quotes taken from previous films or other cultural forms, and a levelling of light and heavy discourses with an utter disregard for hierarchical distinctions between high and low art. Hence, *Pulp Fiction* starts in the middle, unnoticeably backtracks to the beginning of the story and reconnects back to where the film began while its protagonists, two hired killers, talk with the same level of affect or seriousness about McDonald's Quarter Pounders, their last bloody murder and the bible.

In the field of film research, poststructuralism engendered an approach to *genre-as-process*. This approach, heralded by Neale, Altman, Knee and Gallagher, proposed to define genre not according to its recurring elements but rather according to its constantly changing ones. According to Neale, the genre category is mixed to begin with, since genres show *mutability* and variability. Hence he tried to differentiate genres according to their genre mix.[49] Likewise, Altman wrote that 'the process of genre creation offers us not a single diachronic chart, but an always incomplete series of superimposed generic maps.'[50] For Altman, generic shifts occur because syntactic or semantic characteristics taken from other genres are gradually incorporated.[51] A more radical approach was offered by Adam Knee who claimed that while there are attempts to contain genres within 'Iron filings held in position by the magnetic force field of ideology,' genres by their textual nature counter static and essentialist notions.

He then dismissed previous attempts to describe generic evolution by showing that there are so many variables (e.g. natural disasters) that it is practically impossible to account for generic change. Finally, Gallagher dismantled attempts to describe an evolution of the western genre, by showing that all the signs relegated exclusively to later westerns already appeared in early ones.

2.2 POSTSTRUCTURAL INTERTEXTUALITY AND FILM

Similar to the deconstruction of structural tenets and categories, poststructuralists like Julia Kristeva and Roland Barthes (in his later writings) dismantled the attempts to ground textual analyses on Saussurean-inspired semiology. The struggle to discern objective rules determining textual production was not only considered by them to be futile but was also perceived as an ideological attempt to control cultural production. Poststructuralists turned to the dismantling of textual fixtures. They premised that language and other forms of communication are polysemic and multidirectional. Any attempt to fix, stabilize or systematize the process of signification was in their minds an attempt to control human and textual freedom and creativity. Kristeva's and Barthes's notion of textual and human freedom was based upon a conception of a mutating text and an individual: 'a divided subject, even a pluralized subject that occupies not a place of enunciation, but permutable, multiple, and mobile places'.[52] Following Mikhail Bakhtin's literary research, particularly his notion that the meaning of a word in a literary text is not fixed but results from its *dialogical* interaction with various voices and positions within the text, between texts, and in the reader's mind, Kristeva reached the conclusion that it is impossible to apply any deductions made from a presumed language or sign system to manifest textual articulations. Moreover, the whole notion of language as having a priori stable structures was questionable and irrelevant for textual understanding: 'The text, is therefore a productivity, and this means: first, that its relationship to the language in which it is situated is redistributive (destructive-constructive), ... and second, that it is a permutation of texts, an intertextuality: in the space of a given text, several utterances, taken from other texts, intersect and neutralize one another'.[53] Barthes also changed his mind and began to view the text as 'experienced only in an activity of production ... its constitutive movement is that of cutting across ... it cannot be contained in a hierarchy, even in a simple division of genres'.[54] The early semiological view that texts result from a fixed set of rules internalized in an individual's mind and determining the meaning of the text, was exchanged for a conception of the text as intertext: an open set of textual intersections and relations differently realized in each interrelation with a reader or viewer, themselves conceived as having split, shifting identities and entertaining varying positions towards the text. The radical revolutionary-spirited dismantling of the Saussurean linguistic categories used in literary and other cultural research was very productive in the deconstruction of attempts at constituting textual meanings presumed to be reliable, specific and objective. The intertextual approach also generated the postmodern type of textual production, perceived by poststructuralists as constantly evading categorical typologies and subverting them.

Some intertextualists tried to reconstruct a typology of the possible relations between textual segments within a given text or in between texts. Gerard Genette for example, proposed five types of relations: (1) intertextuality: the incorporation within a text of direct quotes from another, plagiarism of another text or allusions made to another text; (2) paratextuality: the relation a text has with its title (e.g. James Joyce's *Ulysses*), prologues or epilogues; (3) metatextuality: the criticizing of one text by another through satire or irony; (4) architextuality: the relation a text has to generic attributions (e.g. romantic comedy); (5) hypertextuality: the adaptation of a text into another medium or its transformation into a different text.[55]

Another interesting intertextual reconstructive attempt was made by Ziva Ben-Porath, who suggested evaluating the relations between texts according to the degree of dependence a *derived* text has to its *originating* text, in terms of the degree of freedom or disorder that the intertextual relation allows readers or viewers.[56] This

Buñuel's *Belle de jour* and Intertextuality

An analysis of Louis Buñuel's film *Belle de jour* (1967) helps to instantiate Ben-Porath's intertextual theory. The film is an adaptation of Joseph Kessel's book written in 1928 and carrying the same title. Buñuel's adaptation would be, in Ben-Porath terms, a 'pseudo-metonymical allusion' to the book. That is, it is dependent on the book in most of its formal and thematic materials, but critiques the book by changing the code determining the combination of materials.

The film, like the book, tells the story of a bourgeois woman (Catherine Deneuve) who loves her husband (Jean Sorel) but is sexually unsatisfied. Following a hint given her by one of their friends (Michel Piccoli), she arrives at a brothel and starts working there during the daytime hours when her husband is busy at work,

finding sexual satisfaction in a series of weird sexual encounters with different clients. However, her guilt feelings towards her betrayed yet beloved husband, along with the chance encounter she has in the brothel with the friend who told her about the place and was surprised to see her there, lead to her having delusions where she is punished for her 'sins'. Things are further complicated when a young and handsome delinquent (Pierre Clémenti) pays a visit to the brothel and falls in love with her. He starts demanding that they meet outside the brothel and when she refuses he arrives at her house. When asked to leave he decides to await the return of her husband and shoots him, an injury that leaves the husband mute and paralysed. Escaping, the delinquent crashes into a car, gets into a shoot-out

led her to place different types of texts along a continuum stretching from highly dependent texts, allowing little freedom in the realization of intertextual relations as in parodies, to highly independent ones such as texts based on metaphorical allusions to others. Among texts in between these poles it is worth mentioning her detection of texts exhibiting an intermediate level of dependence but a high degree of freedom. In this category, termed by her 'pseudo-metonymical allusions', she includes texts that critically revise their originating text. Ben-Porath instantiates the difference of degree in types of intertextual relations by considering the difference between the sentences 'Diana mews like a cat' and 'Diana resembles a cat'. While in the former sentence 'Diana' is highly dependent upon 'cat' and the reader's freedom in the materialization of the intertextual relation is low since only 'meowing' is shared by both texts, in the latter sentence the reader has more freedom since Diana can resemble the cat in different ways such as her having nine lives, her being spoiled or her being infidel.

2.3 CRITIQUES OF POSTSTRUCTURALISM

The poststructural presupposition about textual mutability wrenches away any claim to having found *valid* intertextual relations. This is because intertexts are defined

with a police officer and is shot dead. Sometime later, the 'friend' pays a visit and tells the paralysed husband about his wife's conduct. Following this, the woman loses touch with reality. In the film's final scene the husband rises from his wheelchair and joins his wife for a drink on the terrace from which they see a horse-drawn carriage that figured in the woman's early delusions.

The book's combinatory code is based on a clear distinction between reality and delusion, which supports its distinction between virtuous marital love and immoral sexual desire. Buñuel dismantled the distinction between reality and delusion, thereby collapsing the moral distinction. This he did by unnoticed shifts between reality and delusion. Hence, besides delusions clearly marked as such through disjointed editing and symbolisms, and which occur in a space different than the Parisian milieu of the 'reality' portions of the film (e.g. a disjointed edited scene where the horse-drawn carriage drives her into the woods, she is tied half naked to a tree, mud is thrown over her white dress, and slurs are shouted at her), there are delusions that occur in her regular 'reality' Parisian milieu, edited in continuity (e.g. a scene where the woman sits with her husband and their friend in an outdoor café when all of a sudden the friend breaks a wine bottle and crouches with the woman underneath the table. The husband, who remains seated by the table, says he doesn't understand their murmurings). Likewise, there are delusions that occur in the 'delusional' space but are built like another continuous reality scene where

as multidirectional, shifting and polysemic on all levels. Therefore, any attribution of this or that interrelation between texts, while being subjectively meaningful, is objectively arbitrary. This is perhaps why Barthes described the intertextual process in terms of a non-obliging game while others gave up altogether notions of truth seeking and objectivity.[57]

Overall, while poststructural approaches to genre, author, narrative and text have proved fruitful in deconstructing structuralist or semiological certainties, their perception of a boundless, decentred textual universe in itself generates a theoretical and practical labyrinth. This labyrinth emerges when the impulse that led to deconstruction attempts to reconstruct the concepts it had earlier dismantled. Hence, the above-described poststructural attempts at genre reconstruction made by Neale or Altman are paradoxical. This is simply because the attempt to differentiate genres according to their genre mix, while claiming that genres are always-already mixed, logically demands that they presume *non-mixed* portions that are *then* mixed. But there *aren't* such portions to begin with. Hence, how can someone decide *what* is mixed?

In fact, any perception of texts as constantly shifting configurations of variables is self-contradictory in that it cannot do away at every given point with determining invariables, simply because one cannot specify a difference unless there is something

she meets a new weird client (e.g. a 'realistic' looking and continuously edited scene where she meets in a café a client who asks her to play his dead wife but then calls for the horse-drawn carriage that figured in her delusions, confounding the spectators as to whether the carriage is in 'reality' or they are watching another 'delusion'). A similar confounding of reality and delusion occurs in other registers, such as when characters say things like 'the sun is black today', or when at one point, without apparent narrative reasoning, a shot of the woman's Parisian apartment building is superimposed upon a shot of the woods from her delusions. The final confusion occurs in the last scene where, as noted above, her suddenly rehabilitated husband joins her in their Parisian apartment's terrace, but what they see below is the horse-drawn carriage passing through the woods from her delusions.

Buñuel's change of the book's combinatory code brings down the book's moral and objective distinction between virtuous asexual marital love and punishable debased sexual desire, offering instead a non-judgemental subjective commingling of the two in the woman's mind.

Through these changes Buñuel also allows the spectator a high degree of intertextual freedom in what Ben-Porath would call 'metaphorical allusions'. In what follows, an example of my subjective intertextual freedom is offered. Hence, Buñuel's unnoticed shift between reality and delusion in the film, bordering on surrealism, evoked in my mind Buñuel's and Dali's

constant against which to measure it. Indeed, poststructural reconstructions always posit some such invariable (e.g. Ben Porath's presupposition of an originating text and a text derived from it), but given their basic premises of textual boundlessness and decentralization, they have no good reason to justify its invariability. Moreover, textual boundlessness and decentralization are themselves unjustified invariables.

Countering this widespread poststructural approach were cognitivists like David Bordwell and Noel Carroll. Their approach did not forgo the notion that film constructs are indeed *in* the film rather than subjectively imposed, and that these are usually reconstructed successfully by the minds of coherence-seeking spectators. Cognitivist film constructs are our next concern.

3 COGNITIVIST FILM CONSTRUCTS

The 'cognitive revolution' can be traced back to the 1950s, paralleling the development of computers. This revolution in the comprehension of thought processes tried to understand the way humans acquire knowledge largely by comparing human thought to the way computers analyse and process data. They premised the existence in the human mind of an autonomic level of *mentation* through which humans process information by the manipulation of mental representations such as

earlier surrealist film *An Andalusian Dog* (1929). This interrelation was further consolidated in my mind by the fact that the delusions in *Belle de Jour* are sporadically accompanied on the soundtrack by cat meowing, cow mooing, dog barking and horse neighing. These sounds reminded me of Mauricio Kagel's 1983 score for *An Andalusian Dog*, which included similar animal sounds. In following these intertextual hints, I was reminded that *An Andalusian Dog*, not unlike portions of *Belle de jour*, is totally organized as a dream or delusion in its spatio-temporal leaps, symbols and metaphors, while also dealing with anxieties and uncontrolled sexual desires. However, while *An Andalusian Dog* is a very dynamic, troubling film, *Belle de jour* is overall slow paced and Catherine Deneuve's acting in both 'reality' and 'delusion' is restrained and apathetic. In playing both films in my mind, *An Andalusian Dog* seemed to be *Belle de jour*'s subconscious, laying bare for me the troubled, anxious and turbulent desire lurking beneath *Belle de jour*'s apathetic appearance. Finally, one can find in *Belle de jour* parody in quotations that depend strongly on their originating text and allow for little intertextual freedom. Hence, in the death of the film's charming violent delinquent, Buñuel seems to reference the theatrical death in a shoot-out with the police of the delinquent played by Jean-Paul Belmondo in Jean-Luc Godard's *A bout de souffle* (1960). Also, in both films the delinquents walk along the Champs-Elysées while newspaper vendors call 'Herald Tribune, Herald Tribune'.

symbols, schemes or images, consequently incarnated in different specific symbolic systems. For example, if mental representations of information are numerical, their manipulation is through specific procedures such as multiplication, and their consequent incarnation is in specific symbolic systems like $2 \times 2 = 4$. The cognitivist approach developed in different disciplines such as artificial intelligence, computer science, linguistics, psychology, neurophysiology and anthropology. In psychology, for instance, cognitivists attacked the behaviourist attempt to explain how humans acquire knowledge on the basis of reactions to stimuli. They claimed that behaviourism could not explain how pianists perform since there is no possibility that they react to each tone before playing the subsequent one. It is more feasible to explain the pianist's performance in terms of sets of tones she has arranged in her mind and which she executes successively. In other words, the pianist has a level of mentation autonomous of constant exterior stimulations. Likewise, they rejected the psychoanalytic attempt to explain human manifest and normal ways of thought on the basis of the unknown (i.e. the unconscious) and the abnormal. The complexity involved in the simplest of mental and perceptual processes, such as solving a puzzle, demands research that psychoanalysis cannot provide. They also rejected the psychoanalytic tendency to treat empirical evidence as secondary. Cognitivists strove to verify their findings through empirical research.[58]

They premised that perceptual and cognitive processes follow similar procedures: in general, faced with a phenomenon people raise hypotheses as to its nature based upon previous information stored and organized in their minds, and then proceed to validate their hypotheses. This process is shared by both perceptual hypotheses, which work *bottom up* from sensual data to mind (and which are raised non-consciously or 'automatically'), and by slower, conscious thought processes that work *top down* from mind to perceived phenomenon. For example, in film, cognitivist researchers like Virginia Brooks and Julian Hochberg studied perceptual or bottom-up 'automatic' hypotheses raised by spectators concerning the illusion of three-dimensionality and film movement, as well as their effect upon higher, top-down processes. Brooks researched the influence on top-down processes resulting from spatial and rhythmical disruptions stemming from the transference of live movement to film. She analysed film documentations of dance performances (that deal with movement by their nature) showing how the film inadvertently causes accelerations, shifts in movement and direction, and creates compositional accentuations lacking in the live performance, disruptions stemming from film's two-dimensionality and from editing transitions (e.g. flattening the performance when a group of dancers is shot from above or accelerating motion when cutting between two camera positions on the same dancer). Since these disruptions occur on the perceptual level, spectators cannot consciously control them (as they cannot avoid seeing the projected film in continuous motion or as three-dimensional). In being uncontrolled by spectators, these 'disruptions' overpower top-down intentions. Thus, slowing movement on the perceptual level undermines a top-down intention to impart thematic urgency. Such perceptual disruptions can be seen in the following example:

> We are constantly moving forward
> We are constantly moving forward
> We are constantly moving forward
> We are constantly moving forward

Nevertheless, most film cognitivist research focused upon the top-down processes involved in the comprehension of generic, narrative and stylistic film dimensions. It tried to reveal the schemes, patterns and procedures through which hypotheses are either evoked by films or raised by spectators, and which direct the process whereby spectators construct the film in their minds.

Cognitivism developed in film studies through a critique of the presumptions made by other approaches.[59] Carroll, for instance, rejected in particular the established notions of a film's *immersion* of viewers or its *suspension of disbelief* in their minds, along with the attendant idea that films psychologically or ideologically manipulate passive spectators.[60] Cognitivists offered instead to study the perceptual and cognitive procedures performed by *active* and *aware* spectators in order to comprehend the film flowing before their eyes. Two leading top-down film construct models will be briefly considered in what follows.

3.1 NOEL CARROLL'S QUESTION-AND-ANSWER FILM CONSTRUCT MODEL

Carroll offered a simple and clear model to explain the spectator's way of understanding films. His model was based on the cognitivist presumption that people learn about the world surrounding them by asking questions and searching for answers. Film spectators are no different. The power of movies, particularly Hollywood movies, resided for him in the satisfaction spectators feel when they can phrase to themselves in a simple and clear manner questions concerning the movie playing before them, and receive full answers to these questions, a satisfaction they often lack in real life. In his view, film articulation originally developed to offer such satisfaction.

He argued that the dominant Hollywood trend is totally geared towards this goal, explaining the international popularity of its films. In fact, stated Carroll, the invention of photography and the addition of the illusion of continuity created an easily accessible and understood medium. Moviegoers do not need an arbitrary code, as in written or spoken language, to identify objects or events. Spectators everywhere identify these in very much the same manner that they identify things in the real world. Hence, cinematography is not an arbitrary convention as some semiologists would argue, but a cultural *invention* fitted to human eyesight. Moreover, *point of view* and *shot–counter-shot* constructs, embraced by film as cardinal modes of articulation, are not a complex convention but an easily comprehensible transition based on life experiences. Hence, in life, when someone facing us glances at something, we almost automatically look in the direction, since this was originally a way to identify danger.

Hollywood films, in particular, use movies and the possibilities they allow through framing, composition and editing to raise clear questions and provide full answers. They do so through three basic strategies: *indexing*: drawing attention to something important in the story, as in a close-up showing the spectator that the villain has secretly drawn a gun (why is he doing this?); *scaling*: changing the relations between objects, as when the camera moves away to reveal that the villain is standing behind the sheriff (will he shoot the sheriff from the back?); and *bracketing*: inserting material taken from another context, as when you insert the sound of an off-screen gunshot that kills the villain (who killed him?). In such manner, films also frame the answers to the questions raised, as when a subsequent shot answers the question 'who killed the villain?' by showing up close the sheriff's beloved wife holding a smoking gun, followed by a zoom-out rescaling to reveal her standing on a rooftop overlooking the scene. Carroll went on to specify the types of questions and answers the film raises on its micro-plot level and their relation to the larger questions it raises on the macro-narrative level. While Carroll's model is refreshingly simple and clear it has rightly been criticized for its exclusive laudation of the clarity found in Hollywood films at the expense of more complex or experimental avant-garde films. Also, his focus on film's easily identifiable denoted objects or events was accused of underestimating the complex conventionality embedded in the styling, editing and sound/image manipulations of even the simplest of films (e.g. identifying a peacock in a film-shot and a person in a subsequent shot does not explain the viewer's understanding of the concept of 'vanity' stemming from the juxtaposition of two such shots). These aspects have been addressed by other cognitivists, as will be shown in our next section.

3.2 DAVID BORDWELL'S CONSTRUCTIVIST FILM SPECTATOR

Bordwell's main concern was with the strategies and procedures that allow active and aware spectators to generate hypotheses concerning the film screened before them, and verify or reject these as the film proceeds.[61] He suggested that the hypotheses raised by spectators follow three major different schematic arrangements that they have in their minds:

- *Prototypical schemata* arrange knowledge around a prototypical example as when birds are grouped and classified according to their degree of similarity to or divergence from the sparrow (a chicken, for example, is on the outskirts of the group since it cannot fly).
- *Template schemata* arrange knowledge into different templates such as narrative templates that construe events in causal succession (e.g. exposition, complication, resolution).
- *Procedural schemata* consist of a series of consecutive actions such as the procedure applied when riding a bicycle.

Bordwell's presumption was that spectators strive to construct in their mind a story and a world out of the film screened before them by constantly raising perceptual and cognitive hypotheses and trying to fit the film data into them. Film art in his mind resides in this construction process. The filmmaker presupposes it and construes within the film surprises, distractions, diversions and postponements, which enhance the process of hypothesis generation, verification or refutation. From this, he claimed, derives the film's appeal to spectators. Films, like other art forms, address the cognitive faculties of their spectators and strive to allow them to build a world and a story by realizing these faculties, a process they are hardly aware of, or which is hardly satisfied in real life.[62]

He maintained that the interaction between spectator and film occurs on three levels:

- On the perceptual level, the film imposes upon the viewer the automatic application of perceptual schemes used in spatial or temporal orientation. Hence, three-dimensional schemes determine the generation of hypotheses such as whenever the object is bigger it is also closer, or if the view of an object is partly blocked by another then the former is behind the latter. Likewise, above a certain speed of transition between consecutive still frames with a small difference between what is figured in them, the viewer cannot help but generate the perceptual hypothesis that there is continuous motion between the frames.
- On the level of viewers' previous knowledge and experience, the film triggers prototypical or linguistic schemes that allow them to recognize objects or understand dialogues.
- On the level of the film's construction and film material, the film triggers prototypical film-schemes such as the identification of a 'southern American town' or 'a bank robbery'. Also, the film triggers stylistic film-schemes such as 'following a long shot expect a closer shot', or narrative template film-schemes such as 'exposition, complication, resolution'.

According to Bordwell, spectators are encouraged by the film to raise different hypotheses concerning narrative development.[63] Following Sternberg's delineation of such hypotheses in literature, he mentions curiosity hypotheses relating to what has happened before the film started or after the film has ended, or expectation hypotheses dealing with what will happen next. In general, viewers strive to verify their hypotheses as the film evolves, and tend to hold on to them or refute them according to their plausibility. Viewers use different strategies concerning the verification or refutation of hypotheses such as a 'wait and see' strategy used when evidence is inconclusive. The film on its part uses its own devices to encourage the viewer to raise hypotheses. Suspense films, for instance, encourage the viewer to raise wrong hypotheses or suspend the verification of a hypothesis through intermediary material, raising the level of suspense.

However, contends Bordwell, there are situations where viewers encounter a component in the film that does not fit or re-fit their prototypical or template schemes at all, such as when viewers encounter a duel that has no narrative explanation at the end of a western. In such cases, maintains Bordwell, they turn to generating procedural-scheme derived hypotheses. These aim at offering a *motivation*[64] for such a component. Bordwell distinguishes between four motivational attributions: *compositional*, *realist*, *transtextual* and *artistic*. Hence, viewers may motivate the duel

---

Wrong Hypothesis in *The Silence of the Lambs*

In a scene from *The Silence of the Lambs* (1991) the viewer perceives several shots figuring FBI agents hiding outside a house where they suspect a serial killer is. These shots are alternated with shots of the serial killer inside a house. This triggers in the viewer the stylistic prototype schemes *parallel edited sequence* and *inside/ outside editing transition*, leading the viewer to presume that the whole sequence occurs at the same time in the same location: the besieged house is the one where the killer is. This leads the viewer to raise the hypothesis that the FBI agents are about to break in and a *wait and see* strategy ensues concerning the results of the break-in. The viewer's suspense is raised when one of the officers approaches the door and presses the doorbell, a shot cut to the killer seen reacting to a doorbell ring from inside his house. However, when

compositionally by raising the hypothesis that the film needs a climactic ending, or they may motivate it realistically by saying to themselves that 'such is life, people start a fight for no apparent reason'. Some may offer a transtextual motivation whereby the western genre's conventions demand a duel, while others an artistic one – the duel's choreography fascinated the director.

4 NEO-MARXIST AND PSYCHOANALYTIC CRITIQUES OF COGNITIVISM

Cognitivists have been criticized by Marxists and psychoanalytic film theoreticians for their disregard of the ideological and emotional manipulations of spectators by films. Marxists blamed them for offering a conservative formalism that treats films (and minds) as autonomous constructs. They also critiqued the cognitivist support of films promoting in form and content the ideologies of the exploiting classes.[65] Psychoanalysts blamed cognitivists for their shallow, banal explorations of obvious conscious cognitive procedures on account of the deeper subconscious and emotional lures that films offer spectators.[66]

---

the killer opens the door he sees Clarice, the film's protagonist, whom the viewer knows to be nowhere near the house besieged by her FBI peer agents. These are seen in turn breaking into the wrong house. The viewer's ensuing cognitive shocking surprise results from the film's frustration of one of the editing schemes it has triggered in the viewer's mind. Hence, the film realized the simultaneity portion of the *parallel edited sequence* scheme but not the spatial relation implied in the *inside/outside editing transition* scheme. At this point the viewer generates a new hypothesis concerning Clarice's fate, using a new *wait and see* strategy as to what will happen now that Clarice has to face the serial killer all alone and far away from the FBI officers.

Chapter Summary

Saussure, Semiology, Structuralism and Film Constructs

- Film semiologists based their film-as-signifying-system approach upon Ferdinand de Saussure's key linguistic concepts: the arbitrary relation between signifier and signified; the distinction between language system and speech; the paradigmatic and syntagmatic axes of articulation; and the determination of sign values by their mutual difference from other signs.
- Barthes distinguished between a photograph's *denotative* and *connotative* message to resolve the *photographic paradox*. He claimed that photographic articulations are *mythical* because they *naturalize* meanings.
- Metz discovered a unique film editing system based on arbitrary units (syntagms).
- Wollen imported Peirce's semiotics. He divided the medium into a documentary-indexical dimension, an iconic dimension and a symbolic-conventional dimension.
- Lévi-Strauss's structural method served as the basis for structural analyses of film genres, of films of prominent directors and of films exhibiting similar narratives.
- Structural film analysts use a binary analysis of film's constitutive units to decode the central contradictions dealt with by the films in their deep structure.
- Wright found in Propp a method to discern the structural organization of story developments. He correlated Lévi-Strauss's synchronic analysis with Propp's diachronic analysis in his study of westerns.

Critiques of Semiology and Structuralism

- Poststructuralists critiqued the criteria used by structuralists to define film groupings, film constituting units and the difference between deep and manifest structures.
- Poststructuralists and cognitivists shifted their focus away from the study of the film in itself to the study of the interaction of films with spectators.

Poststructuralism and Film Constructs

- Poststructuralism approaches genre, author and narrative as open process.
- Neale suggested that the genre category is mixed and genres show *mutability*.
- Kristeva suggested that texts are intertexts — open sets of textual intersections and relations, differently realized by readers or viewers that have shifting identities.
- Ben-Porath suggested evaluating the relations between texts according to the degree of dependence a *derived* text has to its *originating* text.

Critiques of Poststructuralism

- The poststructural perception of texts as a constantly shifting configuration of variables is self-contradictory in that it cannot do away with determining invariables.

Cognitivist Film Constructs

- Cognitivists premise the existence of an autonomic level of *mentation* through which humans process information through automatic bottom-up perceptual processes and conscious top-down cognitive processes.
- Brooks and Hochberg studied film-perceptual hypotheses concerning the illusion of three-dimensionality and film movement.
- Carroll and Bordwell tried to reveal the schemes, patterns and procedures evoked by films, through which spectators construct the film in their minds.

Critiques of Cognitivism

- Cognitivism was criticized by Marxists and psychoanalytic film theoreticians for its formalism and its disregard of the ideological and emotional manipulations of spectators by films.

3 DIALECTIC FILM MONTAGE

INTRODUCTION

The concept of dialectic film montage has been used by formalists and cognitivists as a peculiar film device, whose dialectic or rather asymmetrical or contradictory film transitions enhance the viewers' attention to cinematic formal qualities and challenge their cognitive faculties.[1] Structuralists also found affinities between dialectic film montage and their concept of binary oppositions, often searching for contrasting images or editing transitions as drawing attention to or instantiating a film's oppositional binary deep structure.[2] Likewise, some of these theoreticians presumed that cultural systems like film develop dialectically in that new emergent styles and themes strive to exchange those of the canonical works dominating the centre of the system through a struggle with them (i.e. forging their style and themes in dialectic opposition to the canon), eventually replacing the latter.

Notwithstanding these *formal* appropriations of the concept[3], *dialectic film montage* was originally developed as an ideological device by Sergei Eisenstein and other Soviet avant-garde Marxist constructivist filmmakers of the 1920s. It draws upon the Marxist idea of dialectic materialism and concerns an arrangement of film shots in contrasting rather than in complementing or continuous forms, so as to shake or shock rather than appease the spectator. Originally it was aimed at achieving effective propaganda for the Soviet revolution. During the 1960s and 1970s, dialectic montage was used by First World neo-Marxist oriented filmmakers such as Jean-Luc Godard to *deconstruct* the overall continuous and centralizing editing techniques and narrative evolution characterizing Hollywood's film aesthetics. These neo-Marxists perceived the ideological effect of Hollywood films to be the illusory positioning of the spectator as centre and origin of a pseudo-realist developing film, which, by illusorily empowering spectators, led them to conform to the exploitative capitalist system of production. The concept also informs the period's parallel anti-colonial filmmaking or radical 'third cinema', characterized by a desire to communicate with the masses in ways that did not conform to First World modes of communication. Hence, they attempted a *reconstruction* of radical filmmaking by trying to reconcile the non-communicative disjointed audiovisuality and narrative of their peers in the First World with a thematically inverted use of First World genres. Their films were informed by the anti-colonial theories of Frantz Fanon, who unearthed and reassessed sexual, ethnic and racial representations poorly addressed by Marxism. Finally, the widespread 1980s' phenomenon of postmodernism, informed by a dialectic film montage aimed at the *decentring* of text and subject, has posed a dilemma for First World post-Marxists such as Fredric Jameson, while espoused as subversive by parallel postcolonial theorists such as Homi Bhaba.[4]

The following sections consider the evolving figuration of dialectical film montage in the context of Marxist, neo-Marxist, anti-colonial, post-Marxist and postcolonial theories.

I CONSTRUCTIVIST DIALECTIC FILM MONTAGE IN THE CONTEXT OF MARXISM

1.1 KEY MARXIST CONCEPTS

1.1.1 Dialectic Materialism. Dialectic materialism encapsulates the Marxist conception of natural and human essence and their change.

Materialism: Contrary to idealist philosophies, according to which the essence of the world and the power to change it derive from some spirit beyond matter or from human consciousness, materialism maintained that matter is the world's essence and the sole subject of change, and that human consciousness stems from matter and reflects material changes rather than the other way around. Marxism focuses on human material life. As put by Marx and Engels, the forefathers of Marxism:

> The way in which man produce their means of subsistence depends first of all on the nature of the actual means of subsistence they find in existence and have to reproduce. This mode of production must not be considered simply as being the production of the physical existence of the individuals. Rather it is a definite form of activity of these individuals, a definite form of expressing their life, a definite *mode of life* on their part. As individuals express their life, so they are. What they are, therefore, coincides with their production, both with *what* they produce and with *how* they produce. The nature of individuals thus depends on the material conditions determining their production.[5]

Dialectics: Every change results from a constant conflict between opposites that stems from contradictory forces found in all matter. Each material state can be described as a thesis carrying the seeds of its own destruction. In time, these seeds come together to form an antithesis contradicting the initial state. This leads to a collision resulting in a new state, which is a synthesis of the previous states. The synthesis is more than the sum of states that led to it because it includes the relations between and within these earlier states. In its turn this synthesis becomes the thesis of a new state carrying the seeds of its destruction, and so on in an ongoing and widening dialectic process of material change.

1.1.2 Historical Materialism. Historical materialism concerns the Marxist analysis of the evolution of human society according to the method of dialectic materialism:

The exploitative division of human labour as a class division of labour: Humans, from the beginning of their existence and according to nature, produce their means of subsistence in an exploitative division of labour whereby one human uses his power to control and exploit another human and his labour power to enjoy the fruits of labour. Thus, in the primal family the father imposed an organization of labour whereby his wives, children, slaves and animals were his property and laboured for him. This basic primary division of labour, based on exploitation and driven by property accumulation, characterizes the historically evolving and expanding relations of production within and between families, tribes and societies. Hence societies are divided by way of nature along class lines between the exploitative organizers of labour and the exploited labouring classes. Material exploitation is the main generator of the dialectic evolution of human history.

The dialectic expansive evolution of modes of production: Throughout human history people have produced their means of subsistence in different ways. Every mode of production consists of the *forces of production*, that is, the people involved in the production process of a society's means of subsistence; the *means of production*, meaning the machinery, animals and raw materials involved in the production process; and the *relations of production* that exist within the forces of production and between them and the means of production. These relations of production, by way of nature, are based on exploitation. Every mode of production, divided as it is along class lines, is, according to the premise of the dialectic evolution of human history, the thesis whose seeds of destruction stem from the exploited classes. Material changes that impede society's capability to provide its people with the necessary means of subsistence (such as demographic growth or lack of raw materials) lead to an intensification of exploitation of the lower classes and to the growing demand by the latter to change society's mode of production. As such changes accumulate and exploitation intensifies, the exploited classes develop a revolutionary class consciousness that is an expression of the antithesis to the initial increasingly repressive state of affairs. This eventually leads to a revolution carried out by the exploited classes and against the exploiting classes, culminating in a new synthesis that brings about a new mode of production (a new thesis), which, by the way of nature, is exploitative and carries its own seeds of destruction within the newly formed exploited classes. Since humanity is in a constant process of demographic expansion and in need of more means of subsistence, relations between tribes, societies and peoples evolve. These relations lead to the gradual expansion of the production process so that more and more forces and means of production are interrelated and involved in the process of production.

Base structure, superstructure and dialectic materialism: Every mode of production is determined by the material processes of production. These processes comprise the base structure of each mode of production. From this base structure stems a superstructure, which is comprised of the different ways society is organized so that it maintains and reproduces the basic structure of the production of its means of subsistence. The superstructure includes the different institutions and world-views or ideologies needed for the regulation of such task. This is done by way of force (the police, the courts, etc.) and by way of persuasion (ideology). Therefore, according to Marxism, the superstructure is dependent upon the base structure and its sole function is to regulate and facilitate the base structure's process of the production of society's means of subsistence. Hence, in line with the premise of dialectic materialism that change occurs only on the level of the material existence of humans, which finds expression in their consciousness (and not vice versa as idealists would have it), societal change can stem only from the level of the material base structure where exploitation and class struggle take place, and it finds expression on the level of the superstructure. In other words, change cannot stem from the superstructural organization and ideologies in society, since these are determined by the base structure and are a mere expression and consequent regulation of the real processes of change. Only material changes on the base structure engender changes in the superstructure of society and not vice versa.

Superstructure and class struggle: The comprehension of the superstructure as dependent upon and aimed at the maintenance and continuation of the exploitative base structure means that the superstructure primarily serves the interests of the exploiting classes, since they are the ones materially benefiting from this state of affairs. The exploited classes on the other hand, have no real material interest in the continuation of their material exploitation. Therefore, real change can only come from the exploited classes and one of their main targets will be the superstructural institutions and ideologies that serve the exploiters' interests.

The dialectic and expanding evolution of the class struggle: In his study of human history, Marx claimed to have detected a succession of class struggles that brought about changes from one dominant mode of production to another. The major successive struggles were between slaves and masters, vassals and feudal lords, and proletarians and capitalists. Marx maintained that the brutal, dynamically expanding and alienated capitalist mode of production that replaced by necessity the previous feudalist mode of production, will lead necessarily to an egalitarian communist mode of production involving all of humanity in a process of production devoid of exploitation, thus ending the long bloody history of class struggles. The following brief description of the shift from feudalism to capitalism and on to communism instantiates the Marxist theses on the dialectic materialist evolution of human history.

From feudalism to capitalism: The feudal mode of production was primarily agrarian and dominated by the feudal landed aristocracy, which exploited the vassals, who were given land by the feudal lord in return for heavy taxation and allegiance (homage). In time, mostly following epidemics and scarcity, trade developed while many hungry vassals escaped their feudal lords and gathered around trade markets. These mass gatherings of hungry people lacking any trade or know-how 'presupposed'[6] the invention of industrial machines, since these could be operated by unskilled workers and allowed for cheap mass production of goods. Industrialization quickened the development of large cities, which threatened the feudal agrarian mode of production. This process was headed by a new revolutionary class of exploiters, the bourgeoisie (city people) or capitalists, who owned the new means of production and exploited the proletariat, a newly formed exploited class comprised of those who worked on the capitalist-owned industrial machines for a minimal wage. The capitalist mode of production engendered the superstructural state apparatus, an organizing tool able to cope with and regulate the massive, brutal and complex nature of capitalist production. It also engendered the dominant capitalist superstructural liberal ideology that each man is free as an individual. According to Marxism, this ideology primarily functions to safeguard the exploiters' personal capital while persuading the exploited masses that their destiny is in their own hands as free individuals, irrespective of their class positioning within the system of production. This ideology is illusory and allows for the legitimizing of the exploiting classes' material success and the detachment of the exploited individual from his class allegiance and solidarity, by its focus upon his/her personal responsibility for the wretched situation they are in, while offering them a far-fetched promise of personal freedom to gain material success. This new capitalist mode of mass production is based on an unprecedented degree of segregation between the capitalist and the proletarian, mostly due to the wage system, which frees the parties from any mutual attachment or responsibility. This allows for an increasingly brutal form of exploitation along with the development of an alienated and false consciousness among and between the class-divided forces of production. Hence, the proletarian is bound to the capitalist-owned means of production, is concerned with surviving from day to day and is isolated from other proletarians. Therefore, proletarians are alienated from the products of their labour and the real forces that oppress them appear to them to be abstract and beyond their control. The capitalist, in turn, does not labour and receives the finished products of the proletarian's labour. Therefore, capitalists value these products in the abstract, that is, in terms of their exchange value (i.e. their money worth) rather than in terms of their value for the real needs and uses of humans. This situation, whereby the products of labour are abstractly perceived as separated from the labour process, leads to the false, alienating and inverted conception of all human faculties (senses, emotions and thoughts) as objective commodities independent and detached from the process of production. In fact, however, it is this specific process of production that generates such false consciousness.

From capitalism to communism: Marx predicted that the capitalist mode of production would lead by necessity to a communist revolution. He estimated that the logic of capitalist production, based on the brutal dynamics of a mass mode of production driven by a relentless competition to accumulate capital, necessitated ever-growing exploited forces and means of production. This would lead to the rapid expansion and eventual globalization of the capitalist mode of production so that all of humanity would be incorporated into the process, while most of humanity would sink to the ranks of the exploited, given the constant deterioration of their means of subsistence. This expected deterioration, he argued, would be due to the relentless accumulation of capital and the ownership of the means of production by a constantly shrinking class of exploiters. Marx saw in the European imperial expansion into the African, American and Asian continents and the harsh exploitation of their material resources and peoples evidence of the capitalist mode of production's brutal dynamics and eventual globalization. Several contemporary Marxists view today's globalization processes whereby the 'First World' exploits the 'Third World' as further evidence of this process. According to Marx, this capitalist-determined globalization, which will generate a growing disproportion in the class division of labour and ever-harsher exploitation, will forge a revolutionary class consciousness among the proletariat and the classes sinking to its ranks once they realize they 'have nothing to lose but their chains'. This will lead to a worldwide revolution that will destroy the social order, eradicate private capital and institute a truly egalitarian society. It will lead humanity to comprehend that the process of production does not stem from forces beyond their control but is the result of their shared power. Hence, humanity's wilful, conscious cooperation will exchange the previously imposed interrelation. The revolution will dissolve the alienation within the forces of production and between them and the products of their labour, leading to a 'complete emancipation of all the human qualities and senses ... because these qualities and senses have become human, from the subjective as well as the objective point of view. The eye has become a human eye when its object has become a human, social object, created by man and destined for him'.[7]

1.2 MARXISM AND FILM

From the Marxist conception of dialectic materialism and of base and superstructure the Marxist comprehension of film can be derived.

Dialectic materialism and film: Dialectic materialism perceives humans as being in a constant process of material dialectic interaction and change of themselves and of the world of which they are part, changing this world through labour to satisfy their needs. Hence filmmaking can also be perceived as such a process of production whereby from its subject matter or 'content' stems its formal dialectical elaboration. Moreover, according to Marxists, filmmaking should strive to conflate theory and praxis so as to overcome the exploitative division of labour and its attendant alienated false consciousness.

Base structure, superstructure and dialectic montage filmmaking: The Marxist hierarchical division, whereby the material base structure determines the nature and function of the organizational or ideological superstructure, positions film on the level of the superstructure as an ideological apparatus. The film apparatus, which is symptomatic of the base structure, functions to forge an ideological world-view that will persuade people to conform to society's mode of production. The 1917 Bolshevik communist revolution, which led to the establishment of the Soviet Union under the leadership of Vladimir I. Lenin, engendered the cultural *constructivist* revolutionary movement in the arts and in film. Following Lenin's dictum that film was 'the most important art', Marxist filmmakers and film theorists of the period, who saw themselves as working within a society undergoing a change in its mode of production towards communism, rallied to promote through dialectic montage based filmmaking a communist revolutionary mentality. Let us consider the figuration of dialectic montage in the theories and films of two leading Russian revolutionary filmmakers: Sergei M. Eisenstein and Dziga Vertov.

1.2.1 Sergei M. Eisenstein: Dialectic Film Montage as Conflict.
The basic idea informing all of Eisenstein's theory and filmmaking was conflict. He considered conflict to be the mental and artistic reflection of the process of dialectic materialism. He therefore developed a theory of montage according to which the fashioning of each film shot and of the joining of shots in editing has to be based on conflict, that is, on opposition, contradiction or collision. He likened the conflict between joined shots to the collision between thesis and antithesis and their resulting fusion in the spectator's mind to synthesis. Eisenstein's belief in the ontological truth of dialectic

materialism led him to believe that he could forge a revolutionary mentality in his spectators' minds if they processed his films through conflict. Moreover, Eisenstein wanted to control the spectators and direct them towards his goal through conflictual montage configurations that would influence them physiologically, psychologically and intellectually.

Based on this, Eisenstein mounted his shots and joined them along various formal and thematic conflicting parameters, which included graphic conflicts (straight-line shots juxtaposed to diagonal ones), lighting conflicts (lightened versus darkened shots), conflicts in the direction and rhythm of motion (right-to-left movement cut to left-to-right movement), camera distance conflicts (long shots cut to close-ups), camera angle conflicts (high angle cut to low angle), shot crowding (empty-looking shots cut to crowded ones). Through these juxtapositions of brief shots, which had a physiological effect on viewers, Eisenstein forged emotions and ideas.[8]

Eisenstein also used contrasting shots taken from different locations to metaphorically create psychological effects and intellectual ideas. This can be seen, for example, in his likening the massacre of striking proletarians to the butchering of an ox (*Strike*, 1925), or in the ridiculing of the megalomaniac aspirations of Kerensky (the prime minister of the temporary government established in Russia after the ousting of the Tsar and before the Bolshevik revolution), by likening him through conflictual montage compositions to a shining mechanical peacock spreading his metallic feathers (*October*, 1929).

The dynamic conflictual character of Eisenstein's films was aimed at encouraging spectators to feel that the reality alluded to in the films was not given but constructed by the shared power of humans. He therefore objected to mimetic realist

Montage of Conflicts in *Battleship Potemkin*

Eisenstein's most comprehensive and effective use of conflict montage can be found in the 'Odessa steps' sequence of his film *Battleship Potemkin* (1927). The scene consists of a dazzling series of conflicting shots and shot editing that powerfully convey the horror that goes on in the scene where the Tsar's soldiers step in formation down the Odessa stairs while shooting and dispersing a protesting rally of citizens. Notable is the graphic composition of a high-angled tracking

shot showing only the soldiers' aligned and relentless marching feet descending down the stairs (whose horizontal layout is broken by the vertical motion of the soldiers' boots), undisturbed by their stepping over the body of one of the citizens they shot dead, whose graphic unbalanced positioning across several stairs breaks the shot's orderly graphic alignment of camera movement, marching feet and stairs. Powerful also is the series of shots showing a mother carrying

styled films or to the American films based on an illusory continuity and centred upon single heroic individuals. For him, the mere mimesis of reality, the illusion of continuity, and the focus upon individual heroes forge an anti-revolutionary false consciousness according to which the world is given, individuals reign and this order has been established by forces beyond human power. Eisenstein vehemently objected to formalism in film.[9] His conflictual montage was aimed at finding the optimal dynamic rhythm to convey the film's revolutionary content by sweeping over the spectator physiologically, emotionally and intellectually. Mismatches between the montage and the forged subject matter or the spectator's psyche, engendered in his view a formalist, detached experience of the film from 'without'.

As can be seen, the dominant concern in Eisenstein's films and theories was his striving to control the spectators' psyche. This aim seems sometimes to be contradicted by his sporadic mention that dialectic montage forges the spectator's mind 'democratically' since he constructs the film out of opposing views.[10] However, greater than Eisenstein's belief in the spectators' freedom of interpretation was his belief in his power to condition their reactions through film. Evidence for this can be found in his interest in Pavlovian behavioural psychology according to which human behaviour is a result of conditioned reflexes, and in the evaluation of his cinematic montage experiments almost exclusively in terms of their affective influence on spectators. Hence, in a discussion of the '*dynamization of the subject*', not in the field of space but of psychology, i.e. *emotion*' Eisenstein described his own 'harp' sequence in *October* (where shots of those who tried to compromise with reactionary forces are intercut with shots of hands playing harps), as a 'pathological decay … a purely literary parallelism that by no means dynamized the subject matter'.[11] This

---

her dead son in her arms as she ascends the stairs alone to face the descending soldiers until she is also shot dead by them. This sequence powerfully conveys the mother's agony, evoking pity for her and hatred towards the 'machine' like descending soldiers due to its montage editing. Hence, these emotional effects are achieved through the conflictual arrangement of the shots, which cut back and forth from the descending soldiers moving left to right to the ascending mother moving right to left. This alternation, which opposes the shots' movement (up vs down; right vs left) and their figuration (many white uniformed soldiers vs one black dressed woman), also alternates shot distance and angle by cutting from long shots of the soldiers to extreme close-ups of the mother's face and from high-angled shots of the soldiers' feet to low-angled shots of their raised rifles as they shoot the mother, culminating in a close-up of the bullet-wound in her eye.

dominant concern can already be seen in Eisenstein's early writings on film where he values cinematic attractions over thematic concerns, offering to forge such attractions so that they lead the spectator in the direction desired by the director. No wonder that Eisenstein's films were particularly favoured by Goebbels, the Nazi regime's propaganda minister, who asked his filmmakers to produce a 'Nazi *Potemkin*'.[12]

1.2.2 Dziga Vertov: The Dialectics of Film-facts and Rhythmic Intervals. Vertov's neologisms '*kinoks*', '*kinoglaz*' (*film-eye*)[13] and '*kinopravda*' (*film-truth*) were used by him to describe his filmmaking as a dialectic interaction between filmmaker, film technique and material social life, in order to conduct a 'communist decoding of reality'.[14] In Vertov's view, such decoding had to derive from Marxism's perception of humans as being in a constant dialectic process of change (of both themselves and the world of which they are part) through their labour and its derived types of social interactions. Moreover, the filmmaking process had to conflate theory and praxis so as to overcome the exploitative division of labour and its attendant alienated and false consciousness. Without such understanding it is difficult to comprehend Vertov's films. It informs his whole cinematic process of production.

Vertov's 'deciphering' project led him to insist on the exclusive use of documentary shots or 'film facts' as he called them, as well as on filming life 'unawares'. This was derived from his belief that *only* in documentary shots of real-life situations in revolutionary societies can the revelation of truth be carried out. In this he followed Marx and Engels, who wrote that 'the turning of history into world history is not indeed a mere abstract act on the part of "the self-consciousness", the world spirit or

A Communist Decoding of Reality in *Man with a Movie Camera*

Vertov's themes derived from his commitment to a 'communist decoding of reality', as can be seen in his most comprehensive film, *Man with a Movie Camera*. In it, Vertov wanted to 'decipher' the movement and direction of history in the surface appearance of the social life of a city, primarily through the rhythmic interrelation of the labouring processes he documented and their relation to various other aspects of social life. He wanted to show in this way how Soviet society

in his time, despite some remnants of the old order, was harmoniously and collectively producing its means of subsistence. The harmony between workers and their machinery is shown throughout the film in various sequences compiled of rhythmically accelerating shots of different machine wheels rotating, superimposed with shots of skilled workers happily operating the machines. The film also interrelates shots of heavy industry (e.g. electric plants, coal mines) with light industry (e.g.

of any other metaphysical specter, but a quiet material, empirically verifiable act, an act the proof of which every individual furnishes as he comes and goes, eats, drinks and clothes himself'.[15] Vertov drew the line between film fact and film fiction as the first differentiation between truth and falsehood in film. He wrote, 'We engage directly in the study of the phenomena of life that surrounds us. We hold the ability to show and elucidate life as it is, considerably higher than the occasionally diverting doll games that people call theatre, cinema, etc....' and later, 'Stupefaction and suggestion – the art drama's basic means of influence – relate to that of religion and enable it for a time to maintain a man in an excited unconscious state... Away with the fragrant veil of kisses, murders, doves, and sleight of hand!'[16] Vertov constantly compared the fiction film to witchcraft and drugs since for him fiction was nothing but a reflection of ideologies whose function was to turn the spectator away from his awareness of the real processes of production and from truth.[17] He argued that the use of film to imitate life through fiction was an anti-revolutionary violation of real life. He therefore particularly disliked Eisenstein's fictional re-creation of events through documentary strategies, and called for the allocation of funds to documentary rather than fictional films. In shooting, Vertov preferred the use of candid cameras in places where his presence was unnoticed (working places, battle grounds, busy streets) and to position his cine-camera over, under or underneath the objects photographed (as when he dug himself in a hole to shoot a rushing train from below). Only in such manner, he believed, can the filmmaker make 'the invisible visible, the unclear clear, the hidden manifest, the disguised overt, the acted nonacted; making falsehood into truth.'[18] Vertov argued, however, that his inductive

---

cigarette packing, weaving wheels in motion) and with the everyday hustle and bustle of a big city (e.g. trams, buses and pedestrians rushing around), conveying the idea that the various activities simultaneously occurring in different places are all part of the interdependent material fabric of social life. He also interrelated this social fabric to nature's course by correlating the cycle of production with the cycle of life (showing births and deaths) and the cycle of a day (the film's passage from morning to evening corresponds to the passage of people from work to leisure). Within this process Vertov inserted the film worker as he operates his means of production (camera, editing table) aimed not only at 'deciphering' the social fabric but also at inculcating a communal, classless mentality.

approach could bring out the truth in the raw 'film facts' only if it discovered the wider, real material dialectical processes forging each isolated film-fact shot. He thought that these processes could be unearthed through the film editor's search and discovery of the precise dialectical rhythmic 'interval' needed for the interrelation of the film-fact shots, 'to find amidst all these mutual reactions, these mutual attractions and repulsions of shots, the most expedient "itinerary" for the eye of the viewer, to reduce this multitude of "intervals" (the movements between shots) to a simple visual equation, a visual formula expressing the basic theme of the film-object in the best way.'[19] Vertov believed that the rhythm 'revealed' by the editor in his shot juxtapositions embedded the forces with which society's mode of production determines the surface photographed manifestation of social life.[20]

In a way, the film apparatus was for Vertov a true extension of the cognitive and revelatory power of the human senses. This was so because he believed in Marx's prediction that following the communist revolution (as he thought was the case in the Soviet Union) the alienated interaction between humans and machinery is changing into a productive and creative interaction, and that the revolutionary process is freeing the human senses, turning them 'theoretical in practice'. That is why he constantly superimposed the human eye over the camera lenses. That is also why he depicted his own labouring process within the film in its interrelation to other work processes.

The dialectic conflation of man and his tools of labour emblematizing the supersession of their former alienation, found expression also in Vertov's conflation of planning and production (of theory and praxis). This was aimed at effacing the exploitative division of labour and deriving form from matter rather than extraneously imposing form over content the way formalists suggested. Hence he constantly emphasized the need to organize, order and train 'film workers' to the open-ended tasks at hand, as opposed to the precession of the shooting script in the production of the fiction film. However, since the 'themes' he chose for his films were also predetermined and since much information was gathered before shooting, Vertov expanded the notion of documentation to all aspects of the production process, to achieve simultaneity between the various stages of production.

Vertov's objection to work according to pre-planned scripts made it difficult for him to make films after Lenin's death and Stalin's ascent to power. Vertov criticized the growing demand to make films based on scripts that could be supervised by the party apparatus, rightly seeing this as a sign of the bureaucratization of the film industry and of the Soviet Union in general, a trend which Vertov's open-ended filmmaking approach to social life processes could not cope with. Vertov's fears regarding the fictionalization of social life materialized in the rise to dominance of the cultural policy of 'socialist realism' under the Stalinist regime. This doctrine, as defined by Gorki, Zhdanov and Stalin, demanded that artists offer a didactic, easily understood and optimistic picture of socialist reality and the development of the communist revolution. Its translation into practice generated conventional non-dialectic techniques of realist storytelling, depicting social struggles carried out by strong proletarian heroes. One of its most salient proponents was György Lukács, whose views in favour of socialist realism and against experimental art forms were heavily criticized by First World neo-Marxists, particularly by Bertolt Brecht. The emergence of neo-Marxism in the capitalist First World and its approach to dialectic film montage is our next concern.

2 DECONSTRUCTIVE DIALECTIC FILM MONTAGE IN THE CONTEXT OF NEO-MARXISM

The debate between proponents of socialist realism in the Soviet bloc and neo-Marxists in the capitalist First World helped forge the latter's recognition of the need to support the avant-garde and experimental trends in artistic production, vis-à-vis what they perceived as the stiffening formalization of revolutionary art in the Soviet bloc. However, most neo-Marxists also had reservations regarding the practice of a formalist apolitical artistic experimentation in the capitalist world, complementing in their view the widespread popular cultural products that reflected and ideologically promoted the capitalist mode of production. They also recognized a need to view artistic products and their reception in light of psychological and ideological theories. These were used to explain what they perceived as a reflection of a cognitive freezing in capitalist countries, impeding the progressive revolutionary developments that should have stemmed from changes in capitalism's base structure. Whereas Marxism viewed superstructural and mental processes as being dependent upon, and determined by, the material base structure of society, implying that changes stem from the base structure and not the other way around, neo-Marxists developed a comprehension of the superstructural organization and ideologies of the capitalist mode of production as having an autonomous power effectively to block changes in the base structure. This is the cardinal divide between Marxism and neo-Marxism. Moreover, in viewing the superstructure of capitalism as overwhelmingly being in the service of the exploiting classes, neo-Marxists called for its *deconstruction* so as to defrost its powerful blocking of revolutionary trends. In the area of cultural production in general and in film in particular the *constructivist* thrust evident in the dialectic montage based films of Soviet revolutionary Marxists, gradually shifted to a neo-Marxist *deconstructive* approach that called for the use of dialectic montage strategies to lay bare and subvert the dominant capitalist ideological manipulation of the film medium. The first indication of this shift is evident in Walter Benjamin's theses on film, as the following reading of his theses suggests.

2.1 DECONSTRUCTING FILM'S FAKE 'AURA'

In 'The Work of Art in the Age of Mechanical Reproduction',[21] Benjamin offered an interesting thesis on emergent trends in artistic production following the advent of the film medium. Adhering to Marxism, Benjamin considered these trends to be superstructural symptoms of revolutionary sentiments brought forth by crises in capitalism's base structure. Written in 1930s' Germany, Benjamin considered the rise of fascism and Nazism to be the extreme superstructural expression of the capitalist mode of production's attempt to maintain the relations of property in a society on the brink of revolution. He explained that capitalism brings forth an accelerated development of technology that offers means of production capable of satisfying the needs of the exploited masses. However, these technological developments do not serve the demographically growing masses but rather intensify their exploitation by those owning the means of production. This situation generates a revolutionary demand on the part of the masses to change the relations of property. It was in response to this volatile situation that fascism aroused and tried to channel the masses' revolutionary anger to serve its own interests: it enlisted the arts to beautify fascist politics and channelled the masses to war so as to get rid of their excess military technology and what they perceived as expedient human surpluses. As an emergent neo-Marxist, Benjamin considered some of the superstructural artistic trends to autonomously and dangerously serve and support fascist politics.

In tracing the history of society and art, Benjamin contended that the rise to dominance of the capitalist mode of production in the sixteenth century (which placed the entrepreneurs and capitalists as the new exploiting classes) found superstructural ideological expression in the redefinition of the individual as unique, and in the recontextualization of art from an earlier religious ritualistic context to a secular ritualistic one centred on beauty, the unique artist and on art as valuable private property. However, the emergence of powerful revolutionary masses following the technological advances in capitalism placed the individual and the arts within the political context of the mass society. This new contextualization of the individual found superstructural expression, for example, in the development of statistics, a discipline aimed at predicting trends among the masses and implying a shift in the conception of the individual from their being unique (if rich) or meaningless (if poor), to their being meaningful as statistical numbers in a mass. This new mass political context also presupposed and propelled the invention of film, a new art form based on mechanical reproduction and befitting the new mass society. This was because the film, due to its power of reproduction, could be easily distributed and presented to the masses, who now demanded it, whereas the singular and unique work of art couldn't reach them. However, argued Benjamin, this new reproducible art form changed the whole conception of art. He explained this change by adhering to the Marxist idea of the determination of the superstructure by the material base. Hence, the reproducibility of film rendered meaningless the notion of the *material original*, which was the founding concept in the evaluation of the non-reproducible work of art. (It is a contradiction in terms to speak of an *original copy*.) According to Benjamin, up until the age of mechanical reproduction in art, the work of art's unique material existence at a certain time and place was the basis for its conception and its authority. Values such as originality, creativity, eternity, genius and tradition, which together built the superstructural notion of a work of art's 'aura' (defined as an un-crossable distance no matter how close you get), collapsed once the material base founding this aura collapsed. For Benjamin, attempts to adhere to these outdated values in the age of mechanical reproduction were not only faked, but, as will be seen below, dangerous.

Benjamin found evidence of the outdating of 'auratic' values in different aspects of the film medium. Hence, the film actor's performance is not in front of a live audience as is that of the stage actor. Moreover, his acting is non-continuous and determined by the needs of production rather than by the continuous logic of the live staged play. Thus, the real aura engulfing the stage actor and stemming from his singular, continuous performance in front of a live, palpable audience is lost or faked in the fabricated performance of the film actor. Likewise, Benjamin compared the cinematographer to the surgeon in their lack of aura, and differentiated them from the painter whose aura he likened to that of a witch-doctor. This, he claimed, is because cinematographers, like surgeons, destroy their own and their subject's aura in their crossing the auratic distance between them through their analytic, objectifying invasion, cutting and 'editing' of their subject. Painters, on the other hand, like witch-doctors, work from a distance and their authoritative aura is based upon their physical distance from their subject.

In his view, the perception of the reproducible art of film also differed from that of the unique work of art. The latter pulls the viewer towards it because of its authoritative unique existence in a certain time and place, and its appreciation is based on detached meditative contemplation derived from such authority. The reproducible film, however, lacks a unique singular existence and therefore loses its authority and rushes towards the viewer, who often perceives it absent-mindedly.

Also, Benjamin contended that the historical depth stemming from the unique work of art was flattened in the reproducible film due to its being a copy with no original and its potential for projection at any time and space.

Hence, the characteristics of the film medium – freedom from time and space constraints, instantaneousness, multiplicity and lack of authority – befit the age of the masses on the verge of revolution, who strive for freedom and equality.

However, Benjamin feared that the mass-political context leading to the emergence of film, as well as the medium's peculiar and specific characteristics might fall prey (against the will of the masses and film specificity) to political movements that object to the masses' interest in changing the relations of property. According to Benjamin, the widespread notion of 'art for art's sake', which evolved following the crisis in the arts brought about by film, was inadvertently a dangerous supporter of such political forces, particularly of fascist politics. This was because the 'art for art's sake' profession that art is devoid of any sociopolitical context was unaware of the compulsive political context in which art found itself in the age of mechanical reproduction and the mass society. Therefore such a view of art not only encouraged political disengagement that aided the interests of those who wanted to divert the masses away from political action, but ultimately ended up serving fascism. This was because this perception catered to the fascist interest in enlisting the arts to offer the masses a way to express their frustration without serving their interest in changing the relations of property. Fascism did so by enlisting the values of auratic art – genius, eternity, originality (values that were outdated with the advent of reproducible art) – to beautify its brutal politics. Fascism spuriously related these auratic values to entities like race and leader through their beautification in fabricated reproductions. Fascism's aim was to devoid the masses of what film technology allowed: to represent themselves and their interests. Instead, it fabricated a fake beautifying aura of a total social order where the 'original' people parade before the 'genial' fascist leader. Moreover, by particularly beautifying an 'eternal' war, fascism channelled the revolutionary aspirations of the masses towards their self-destruction.

Hitler's Fake Aura in Riefenstahl's *Triumph of the Will*

Leni Riefenstahl's Nazi propaganda film *Triumph of the Will* (1935) is an emblematic expression of the aesthetization of politics practised by fascism. The film, documenting the Nazi party convention in Nuremberg in 1934, repeatedly shows the orderly military march of the Nazi legions along streets populated by large cheering crowds. These shots are intercut with repeated empowering low-angled images of Hitler as he

As against these trends Benjamin offered vague suggestions concerning the use of film for purposes that would serve the true revolutionary aspirations of the exploited masses and would deconstruct the auratic fabrications of fascist filmmaking. Hence, for Benjamin, the cine-camera's capability to document reality objectively and analytically, along with its power to distribute these images on a large scale, allowed for the representation of the life of the masses and of their surroundings. In such ways film could help the masses get acquainted with each other and with their life constraints, while also showing them points at which such constraints could be overcome. He attributed this to the film medium's capacity to explore reality through slow or fast motion, which he compared to psychoanalysis's revelation of the human unconscious or to the surgeon's scalpel operation on the human body. Like Vertov's belief in the *film-eye* (see p. 78), Benjamin believed that films, in their being unconfined to a single place and time, could reveal processes hidden from the human eye.

Benjamin also suggested that film should be used to train the masses' cognitive abilities so that their awareness is sharpened, preparing them to face the dangers of the complex and volatile life in the age of mechanical reproduction. He offered to exchange the outdated 'auratic' art paradigm of perception through contemplative immersion, with the old architectural paradigm of absent-minded tactile perception through skilful habitual use. Film, by its nature, conducted tactile assaults on the viewer due to its constant jumps in camera point of view, angle, time and location. This constant change could raise the viewer's awareness in face of these 'shocking' attacks. Moreover, through its tactile attacks, film could train the masses to develop habits that could free their minds to face further challenges (as when you drive a car, where you habitually perform complex operations while freeing your mind for further activities).

Benjamin's position implied that film should enhance its jumpy nature to be dialectically confronted by an aware viewer, and not yield to the practice of fabricated 'auratic' films that strive to ease the film transitions and overwhelm their audiences.

---

enthusiastically preaches to the ordered legions facing him, or as he shakes the hands of cheering crowds in the streets. Thus the film centres the cheering crowds and the legions around Hitler's charismatically fabricated image, the same crowds and legions he will soon lead outside the film, in reality, to an atrocious war.

In this, Benjamin's position resembles Eisenstein's conflictual montage theory, although his aim was not to control the viewers' mind (which is what Eisenstein wanted in his *film-fist* approach) but to enhance their awareness to the machinations of the film apparatus.

Benjamin's theses translocated Marxist theories of film to the capitalist First World. In the process, these theories underwent changes due to the fact that 'theses about the art of the proletariat after its assumption of power or about the art of a classless society would have less bearing ... than theses about the developmental tendencies of art under present conditions of production.'[22]

Benjamin, like the revolutionary Russian filmmakers, viewed film as a super-structural ideological expression of changes in the base structure, whose function is to forge a revolutionary consciousness in a society on the verge of revolution. He also viewed the First World apolitical artistic avant-garde ('art for art's sake') as promoting anti-revolutionary ideological tendencies in the same way as earlier Marxists criticized formalism in the arts.[23] Unlike them, however, he conceived art as having the autonomous and effective power to ideologically interpret changes in the base structure that may contradict the progressive march of history and halt or even change its course.

Benjamin's theses formed part of the growing focus of neo-Marxists in the First World upon the functioning of ideologies and of art as ideology in society. The notion that ideologies may be autonomous from the material base had serious repercussions for the materialism that founded Marxist theory. However, neo-Marxists found it hard to cling to the Marxist idea that ideologies are a mere reflection of changes in the material base structure.

2.2 NEO-MARXISM AND IDEOLOGICAL APPARATUSES

A central concern of neo-Marxists in the capitalist First World was the apparent fail-ure of Marx's prediction that a world proletarian revolution would occur by necessity, given the relentless expansion of the brutal capitalist mode of production. Stalin's policy of the containment of socialism to the Soviet bloc and the growing strength of capitalism in the First World led them to ponder on the reasons that impeded a communist revolution in the First World. Antonio Gramsci, an Italian communist jailed by the Fascists in 1926 where he remained for twenty years (almost until his death), developed in his *Letters from Prison*[24] the idea that capitalism's survival derives foremost from the superstructural cultural-political *hegemony* of the ruling classes. No social order, he maintained, can survive without social legitimacy based upon a wide social consent. He therefore reached the conclusion that capitalism persists not because it is not materially exploitative or brutal but because the ruling classes manage to *persuade* the ruled classes that the mode of production exploiting them is natural and even desirable. In his view, changes in the base structure that should lead to revolution do not find expression in the superstructure because the cultural-political hegemony of the ruling classes brainwashes the minds of the exploited masses. A similar conclusion was reached by members of the Frankfurt School, whose critical theory maintained that the widespread popular culture in the capitalist West was a *culture industry* pumping capitalist ideologies into the heads of the exploited. This neo-Marxist approach was developed into a solid and very influential theory of ideology during the 1960s by French philosopher Louis Althusser.

According to Althusser, Marxism undervalued the autonomous functioning of ideologies and understood them 'like the ... dream among writers before Freud',[25] that is, as a weightless reflection of material changes. Therefore, Marxists wrongly maintained that changes in the base structure lead by necessity to homologous superstructural changes. In 'Ideology and Ideological State Apparatuses',[26] Althusser claimed that Marxism overlooked the functioning of the superstructure in thwarting the revolutionary process and enabling the continuation of the capitalist mode of production. He therefore set out to explain how this occurs. He reached the conclusion that this happens because of the superstructural state apparatus, which coordinates between *repressive* state apparatuses and *ideological* ones. While repressive apparatuses (police, army, censorship, courts, jails, etc.) maintain the social order through force, ideological ones (the education system, the mass communication system, the family institution, etc.) do so by persuasion. He maintained that without effective ideological apparatuses the social order would collapse and revolution would ensue, mostly because repression by force would intensify given the growing unrest of the exploited masses. Therefore Althusser reached the conclusion that the major factor thwarting revolution is the ideological state apparatus that persuades the exploited masses that the mode of production exploiting them is right and necessary. Hence, as long as these apparatuses are not deconstructed, there won't be any need for the forceful repression that will hasten revolution. Having reached this conclusion, Althusser searched for the mechanism by which ideologies persuade people to operate against their material interests. He started by rejecting widespread definitions of ideology, in particular the claim that it is a twisted representation of reality. Hence people say of others that 'they represent reality to themselves in a twisted manner' or, often when speaking of their past, they say, 'I used to have a twisted representation of reality but now I see things clearly'. Why, he asked, would people represent to themselves their reality in a twisted manner if they assume by that very definition that reality can be represented in a straightforward manner? His reply to this question was that these definitions of ideology fail because they are based on the misleading presumption that people can *choose* to represent their reality in a straightforward way. He therefore reached the conclusion that ideologies are not chosen but given to people and that their persuasive power derives from the illusion they give people that they have *chosen* to believe in the reality depicted by a given ideology and that they are the ones constituting this ideological representation of reality of their own free will. Hence, concluded Althusser, ideologies operate by twisting the *relation* that people have to their reality, a twisting having to do with the *illusion of choice*. This illusion is what allows for ideological persuasion since if people perceive the ideology given to them as their own choice, they willingly submit to its representation of reality and willingly perform the duties it imposes upon them.

According to Althusser, the factor through which people are manipulated into 'choosing' is the notion of their being *subjects*. The concept of the subject, he said, aptly has a double meaning: on the one hand, it refers to someone who is free to choose and take decisions; while, on the other hand, it implies submission, the state of being subjected to something or someone else (as when we speak of a king's subjects). Hence, ideology operates by 'turning people into subjects'. This is achieved by ideology's appropriation of a person's selfhood. In fact, said Althusser, from the moment we have selfhood we are 'always-already' subjects of this or that ideology. In order to explain the conflation of subject and self Althusser relied on the theory of selfhood developed by the psychoanalyst Jacques Lacan.[27] Lacan hypothesized that a human's first notion of self results from his/her seeing themselves *reflected* in other humans or, wherever available, in their mirror image. Hence, he argued that between the ages of six and eighteen months, when human motor coordination lags behind a well-developed sense of sight, the child identifies his/her reflection in others or in mirrors as separate, independent, whole and coordinated. The gap or contradiction between this initial identification with our reflected image and our deficient coordination, perceived as lack, is what determines our relation to selfhood throughout our lives. Hence, we will strive throughout our lives to fill this felt gap between our inner sense and the full image appearing in our outer self reflection. According to Lacan, this is also the basis for our imaginary identification with others. Of particular importance for Althusser was that this initial sense of self is based upon a reflection in our minds of a detached image that does not correspond to our sensed material referent. Althusser's claim was that ideology, in its appealing to our selves, reconstitutes in us the sense of this imaginary self and suggests that we can attain fullness if, as free independent subjects, we choose to emulate the fuller ideal Subject (with capital S) offered by an ideology. In turn, our identification with this imaginary ideal Subject suggests that if we strive to see the world from its point of view we will attain the desired fullness in our lives. In turning individuals into subjects through their notion of selfhood, ideology performs a reversal whereby people's material existence becomes abstract while their ideological imaginary becomes their reality.

At this point Althusser asked what is this ideal Subject reflected in a person's mind and making him/her strive to be its replication? His answer to this question returned the apparent abstract discussion of ideology to Marxist materialism. Althusser claimed that the ideal Subject is nothing more than the sum of qualities and actions needed to be performed by concrete individuals for a given mode of production to operate optimally. In the capitalist mode of production these attributes are geared towards the extraction of maximum profit for the owners of the means of production. Hence, whenever an individual is involved in a certain apparatus of production (be it an electric plant, a supermarket or a music concert), that apparatus's ideal Subject begins, through the individual's notion of selfhood, to figure in the individual's mind when he performs the apparatus's rituals and actions. Identifying with the ideal Subject and its attendant promise of self-fulfilment leads the individual to help the apparatus to maximize its profits through him/her. Thus, out of 'self-conviction' people cooperate willingly with the production mode extracting profit from them. Usually, said Althusser, the ideological apparatus succeeds in subjecting individuals to willingly cooperate. However, when the ideological apparatus fails (often because individuals may be subject to a different ideology), the repressive apparatus comes to the fore to 'put them back in place' and to 'restore order'.

Althusser went on to say that every repressive apparatus has an ideology. Hence, the repressive army apparatus has an ideology aimed at persuading its targets to perform willingly duties that are normally violently imposed, and the jail system tries to persuade convicts that good behaviour is good for them. For example, if an individual receives a letter addressed to him/her from the internal revenue service calling him/her for assessment, the ideal 'tax-payer Subject' starts to figure in his/her mind. If the individual is not subject to a different, opposing ideology then he/she will strive to be a 'good subject' and emulate the ideal tax-payer Subject by organiz-ing his/her bills, checking expense reports and, being sure of the benefits that paying revenues bring to society, he/she will willingly pay the dues imposed upon him/her. If the internal revenue service ideology functions, that individual will feel that it is out of his/her choice and power that the service is instituted.

Just as repressive apparatuses that operate mostly by force have a minor ideo-logical dimension, so ideological apparatuses that operate mainly by persuasion have a minor repressive dimension. Hence, the state educational ideological apparatus has punitive measures in case pupils are not persuaded to study, while the state communication ideological apparatus imposes censorship if its creative subjects 'cross' moral or political lines. In sum, ideology operates by turning individuals into subjects, thus persuading them that it is out of their own free choice that a given production mode operates. In such manner ideology twists the relation individuals have to their real conditions of existence. Rather than viewing their position in society as imposed upon them, they believe that they have chosen to be there.

Furthermore, while different ideologies express the material interests of different classes in a given mode of production, these are subsumed under the dominant ideology expressing the interests of the ruling classes. This dominant ideology constantly and through various means and venues portrays the picture of a reality that serves the ruling classes. This picture of reality is adopted by the ruling classes, but also, in its 'contradictions', by the ruled classes as well. In such manner the exploited are led to believe that each one of them is responsible for his wretched situation, has chosen it and even constitutes it by his own free will.

This conception, attributing to dominant ideological apparatuses a cardinal role in the preservation of the capitalist mode of production, led Althusser to call for the deconstruction of the reality portrayed by its ideologies through the deconstruction of the processes constituting the subject in these dominant ideologies.

2.3 FILM AS AN IDEOLOGICAL APPARATUS AND DIALECTIC MONTAGE AS ITS DECONSTRUCTION

Neo-Marxist film theoreticians and filmmakers were highly influenced by Althusser's theory of ideology. Viewing film as an ideological apparatus, they tried to discover how films turn viewers into their subjects and hence persuade them not only that the reality portrayed is a desired one they are invited to choose as their own, but that this reality could not exist without their own constitution of the film.[28] Jean Louis Baudry, for example, searched for the 'Ideological Effects of the Basic Cinematographic Apparatus'.[29] His claim was that the invention of film derived from modern capitalism's need to reinstate in people the illusion of their having control over their own lives, an illusion needed for their willing cooperation with a mode of production that in fact has stolen away any remains of such self-control. Hence he found in the film apparatus itself ideological effects that constitute a 'transcendental' subject willing to cooperate with the capitalist mode of production.

He argued that the film-viewing situation encourages an idealist, non-material version of reality by likening the viewer's situation to that described by Plato in his cave metaphor. According to Plato, people's perception of reality resembles that of chained prisoners sitting in a darkened cave and forced to watch on the wall facing them projected images that are a mere degraded reflection of the world of true ideas, without their being able to turn around or leave the cave (except for the philosopher). This astounding Platonic premonition of the film-viewing situation was taken by Baudry to elucidate his claim that films encourage a vision of a reality whose essence is spiritual and transcendental rather than material. He then went on to show how the different components of the film apparatus further constitute this 'transcendental' subject, persuading him/her to cooperate willingly with the capitalist mode of production. Following others, he began by arguing that the camera lenses, based as they were on the fifteenth-century Renaissance invention of linear perspective (an invention from the beginnings of the capitalist mode of production), adapted the ideological effects of this invention to modern capitalism. Hence, Leon Battista Alberti's invention of linear perspective (*perspectiva artificialis*) renders an illusion of three-dimensionality by organizing the space of a painting within a rectangular frame so that the overall line directions converge into one point, which he termed the 'vanishing point'. The location of this point in the canvas converges with that of the eye-level of a presumed average spectator from whose point of view the painting is to be looked at. Thus, a spectator who assumes the position prescribed by the painter whereby his/her eye overlays the painting's vanishing point, experiences the full illusion of depth. According to Baudry, this deployment has a clear ideological effect since, in ideological terms, the painting organizes a homogenous, centred and hierarchically organized space that appears to emanate from one originating point or to converge into it. This originating point is that of the painting's ideal viewing Subject, whose point of view a concrete spectator assumes. In such manner the perspective painting constitutes its spectator as subject: he is positioned at a certain point that lets him experience himself as the point to which all the illusory deep space deployed converges, or as the origin from which it emanates. Baudry went on to claim that the cine-camera, based on linear perspective, enhances this ideological effect since the cine-camera's point of view, which the viewer identifies as his own, can move over a continuous deep space. This continuous movement is achieved according to Baudry by means of another ideological manipulation that exists in the film-strip projection speed. Hence, because of a limitation in human vision, beyond a certain speed the viewer's eye cannot perceive the film strip's discrete images, leaving him no choice but to experience these in an apparent continuous flow. In such manner the ideological subject constituted by the cine-camera and projector is further 'transcendentalized'. This subject assumes the unprecedented illusory power to perceive as his own constitution a centred, homogenous and hierarchically organized space that he/she can now control by floating over or across it.[30]

Nevertheless, Baudry contended that editing the film shots together carries a potential subversion of the ideological effects of the camera lenses and the film-strip projection, since each shot transition may make the viewer aware of the fact that the reality depicted is not under his control and that someone or something else is changing the set-up. This potential subversion was, according to Baudry, what motivated the evolution of continuous editing. In his view, continuous editing, whose main function is to hide shifts in camera positioning from the viewer's attention, ends up reinforcing the film's ideological effects. In order to ground this conclusion Baudry enlists the phenomenological philosophy of Edmund Husserl. Husserl describes a thought process that can offer a viable explanation for the way in which continuity editing consolidates the position of the viewer as ideological subject. According to Husserl, since our sense data provide us with mere segments of a sensed object at any given time (e.g. we cannot simultaneously see an object's front and behind), we derive our sense of selfhood from the partial data provided by our senses because something has to deduce the object's fullness as it appears in our mind. That something, says Husserl, cannot but be our selfhood. Therefore, concludes Husserl, the moment we constitute the object is the moment we constitute our selves. Baudry used Husserl's theory to explain how *continuity editing*, in its way of chaining together the partial data provided by shot segments, reinforces rather than subverts the viewer's sense of selfhood by the ideological illusion that she constitutes these film segments into a whole. These ideological effects of the film apparatus, claimed Baudry, precede and enable the secondary manipulations of a specific ideology in a given film or the viewer's identification with the film's stars. The conclusion reached by Baudry, and other Althusserian film theorists and filmmakers, was that there was a dire need to deconstruct the subject-positioning process of the film apparatus, so as to subvert its manipulation of viewers into a willing acceptance of, and desire to emulate, the ideological reality screened before them. In their view, this could be achieved primarily by the use of the non-continuous and conflictual strategies of dialectic montage to deconstruct the illusion of continuity, centredness and coherence constructed by films and constituting ideological subjects. Once the viewer becomes aware of these manipulations through such deconstructing montage

Dialectic Deconstruction in the Films of Jean-Luc Godard

The film director who outlined the cinematic paradigm of neo-Marxist dialectic deconstructive montage is Jean-Luc Godard, whose dictum 'if you want to say something different you have to say it differently' generated an impressive body of work, including the films *Masculine/ Feminine* (1966), *Made in USA* (1966), *La Chinoise* (1967), *2 ou 3 choses que je sais d'elle/Two or Three Things I Know About Her* (1967) and *Weekend* (1968). Godard's films constantly destroy character, narrative, and temporal and spatial coherence. This is coupled with a deconstructive analysis of dominant cinema styled shots and sequences, laying bare their presumed ideological manipulations of beauty and of human emotions. This is often complemented with a voice-over offering Marxist analyses of the social structure in the capitalist First World and its resulting cinematic image of reality. For instance, in a scene from *La Chinoise* (discussed in formalist terms in Chapter 1) the characters add a

strategies, the film lays bare its ideological manipulations and loses its ideological power.

Stephen Heath,[31] for example, analysed such deconstruction in Nagisa Oshima's film *Death by Hanging* (1968). In this film, Oshima lays bare through the film's content the ideologically based procedures of the legal system while deconstructing its continuity through dialectic montage, thus preventing the viewer's falling prey to the film apparatus's ideological effects. *Death by Hanging* tells the story of R, a murderer sentenced to death, who has lost his identity after surviving his execution. Since R does not know who he is, he cannot be executed again until he regains his sense of identity, for otherwise he cannot be held responsible. The film follows the attempts of 'correction officers' to help R regain his identity so that he can be executed again. The film's problematization of the concept of the legal subject through R's amnesia destabilizes the viewer's notion of identity. However, this destabilization is mainly achieved through the difficulty viewers find in trying to unify and make coherent the film's spatial, temporal and narrative deployment, which Oshima constantly dismantles.

3 RECONSTRUCTIVE DIALECTIC FILM MONTAGE IN THE CONTEXT OF ANTI-COLONIALISM

The neo-Marxist conception of ideology and of film as ideology was harshly criticized by Third World Marxist oriented anti-colonialist theorists and filmmakers. Their critique was that because of their location in the heart of capitalism's developed

---

romantic musical score on a gramophone to accompany the repetition of a conversation on the politics of language they just had. In this scene, Godard not only makes the viewers conscious of film form and technique as formalists would have it, but he primarily lays bare how dominant cinema manipulates our emotions by showing how a political conversation loses its explicit meaning and changes into a romantic emotional sub-textual interchange once the musical score is added.

In another shot, showing a symmetrically arranged French bourgeois living room, a dialectically opposed written graffiti on the wall reads 'We need to fight ambiguous words with clear images,' thus deconstructing the dominant cinema's manipulation of composition and beauty to promote its world-view.[32]

countries, neo-Marxists reached a theoretical and practical dead-end and failed to identify the palpable revolutionary trends among the peoples of the Third World. The neo-Marxist deconstructive approach led, in their view, to nothing but an ongoing sense of frustration, expressed in uncommunicative films aimed at the intellectual elites and totally detached from the exploited masses. As against this, anti-colonialists saw their underdeveloped societies as being on the verge of revolutions that might or might not be communist, but which in any case should be advanced so as to liberate their peoples from the racist, cultural and economic repression that the colonial or neo-colonial regimes exercised in their exploitation of those called by Frantz Fanon *The Wretched of the Earth*.[33]

They were strongly influenced by Fanon's anti-colonial theories. He unearthed ethnic, national and racial concepts claiming that the Marxist focus on the material analysis of a generalized human class struggle overlooked or dismissed the significance of such concepts to considerations of exploitation. Fanon emphasized the need for, and legitimizing of, a colonized *spontaneous* revolutionary and liberating avenging *violence* stemming from Third World peoples' wretched situation. This led him often to position his non-essentialist yet politically functional constructions of race, nation and culture over and above economic material determinants. As Fanon put it, 'In the colonies the economic substructure is also a superstructure. The cause is the consequence; you are rich because you are white, you are white because you are rich. That is why the Marxist analysis should always be slightly stretched every time we have to do with the colonial problem'.[34] However, this stretching often resulted in the over-valuation of the cultural and racial dyads of East/West or Black/White over the First/Third or North/South world materialist economic dyads. Hence,

Anti-colonialism in Pontecorvo's *Battle of Algiers*

An emblematic example of the power and fallacies of the anti-colonial approach in film can be found in Gillo Pontecorvo's highly acclaimed film *Battle of Algiers* (1964). The film, which depicts the ultimately successful anti-colonial independence struggle carried out by the Algerian 'Front for National Liberation' (FLN) against the French settlers and army, offers a sweeping First World war-documentary genre depiction of the violent and bloody struggle that went on, while siding with the Algerians. This is achieved by inverting the usual figuration of heroes and villains in the war-documentary genre, figuring the colonized Algerians as heroes and the French settlers and army as villains. However, in its inverted content but straightforward use of the genre, and probably because of it, the film fails to couch the struggle within the framework of an economic-political class struggle. Instead, it ends up focusing upon the cultural and racial differences between colonized and colonizers as grounds for its support of the Algerian war of liberation. This comes through, for example, in

Fanon's and other anti-colonial theories often implicitly supported nationalistic and even racist anti-colonial or anti-white revolutionary trends, whose relation to the Marxist materialist analysis of capitalism was poorly developed. As Fanon wrote, 'Decolonization unifies that people by the radical decision to remove from it its heterogeneity and by unifying it on a national, sometimes racial, basis'.[35]

Fanon's strategy called for the identification of revolutionary trends, the exploitation of the revolutionary potential found in local myths and indigenous cultures so as to better communicate with the exploited masses, and the incorporation of the class struggle within the struggle for national liberation and independence.

Fanon's influence is evident in the 1960s' wave of anti-colonialist films coming out of Third World countries or dealing with the situation from such a view-point.[36] Most of these films, each in its peculiar way and within its specific national context, tried to channel the portrayal of the harsh living conditions of the poor and their cultural myths towards revolution. Ousmane Sembene's *Xala* (1975), for instance, figured an indigenous curse that causes sexual impotence called Xala as a revolutionary agent. Xala is used to critique and punish a Senegalese political leader who becomes an accomplice of First World neo-colonialism, and who uses the bribes he receives from French officials to gain financial and sexual privileges from the poor. The Xala curse put upon him causes him sexual humiliation vis-à-vis the second young wife he takes, leading to his rolling in the streets asking bystanders to urinate on him so that he can get rid of the curse.

On the level of form, the anti-colonial filmmakers' attempts to follow Fanon and conflate the essentially Marxist anti-nationalist class struggle with national independence struggles, translated into a mixing of dialectically disjointed

---

a scene where three women belonging to the FLN are making preparations to cross over into the French part of the city of Algiers to plant bombs in different civilian locations, as an act of retaliation for an earlier bomb detonated by the French in the besieged Kasbah (the Arab Quarter in the city). In the scene we see the women in front of a mirror, shedding their veils, cutting or dying their hair to look French and putting on Western-looking dresses. The scene is based on a dialectic montage editing of shots of the women taken from different angles, accompanied by accelerating Arab-style drumbeats. What transpires, however, in this montage edited process of 'deconstruction' and 'reconstruction' of the women's identity is the radically different physiognomy of the women that still remains accentuated after they disguise as 'French', hence insinuating that the bloody national liberation struggle stems from cultural and racial discrimination rather than from economic-political exploitation.[37]

audiovisuality and narrative with a contradictory trend aimed at reconstructing the highly efficient and manipulative First World film genres.

This is particularly evident in Glauber Rocha's Brazilian films. Rocha developed the notion of a 'cinema of hunger', claiming that films with poor production values and disjointed audiovisuality homologously replicate the wretched life conditions and confused mentality of the exploited poor. In his film *Anthony of the Dead* (1968), for example, he tells the story of a legendary professional killer, hired by a landowner to eliminate messianically driven rebelling peasants, who ultimately turns against the landowners. The film is an intentionally badly made rendition of an American western (a genre popular in Brazil), using slow-paced disjointed sequences figuring symbolic figures representing different classes, whose acting and dialogues are in 'quoted' Brechtian style, and referencing popular mythical Brazilian figures and indigenous rituals. However, Rocha's use of the popular American western genre and indigenous myths to articulate a revolutionary class struggle that will presumably communicate with the exploited masses subverted his own intention. By using the western genre in a Godardian 'deconstructive' style, Rocha laid bare the genre's ideological manipulations but also destroyed the appeal of the film to its intended audience. The film was also somewhat misguided in its presentation of the messianically driven peasants as doomed ignorant victims led by delirious leaders, who need the violent intervention of a mercenary whose actions stem solely from a desire for revenge against his former masters.

Postmodern Split Narrative in Lonze's *Adaptation*

Postmodernist levelling of different ideological positions can be seen in the split narrative of Spike Lonze's film *Adaptation* (2002). The film develops as a stream of consciousness, disjointedly edited film, telling the story of Charlie Kaufman (Nicolas Cage) who is a screenwriter repelled by the way he looks and extremely unsure of himself. He has a twin brother, Donald, who is his opposite. Donald is self-assured and when he decides to become a screenwriter like his brother, he comes out with a script loved by Charlie's film agent. Whereas insecure, repelling Charlie is interested in a non-eventful *stream-of-consciousness* film like the one the viewers are watching, Donald is interested in the generic, causal, conventional development of a story, with protagonists who evolve and change throughout the film following their overcoming of a difficult task involving action, drama and tension. Charlie, contracted to adapt a book into a film gets lost in the labyrinth

4 DECENTRED DIALECTIC FILM MONTAGE: POSTMODERNISM, POST-MARXISM, POSTCOLONIALISM

The ascent of postmodernism to cultural dominance during the 1980s challenged neo-Marxist theories of deconstruction. The attributes of the postmodern text – segmentation, character split, spatial and temporal decentring – perceived by 1960s' and 1970s' neo-Marxists as revolutionary tropes leading to textual freedom and social equality, suddenly became the dominant trend in First World capitalist cultural production. In the 1980s, post-Marxists began to realize that the postmodern shattering of hierarchies and boundaries between high and low art, the levelling of different styles and historical periods, and the understanding of the text as an intersection of endless textual references, do not lead to more real freedom and equality. They reached the conclusion that the cultural pluralism of the postmodern text was not a progressive expression in the superstructure of changes in the base, but rather a regressive superstructural expression of the base structure of globalizing capitalism. To paraphrase Walter Benjamin's view on fascism, post-Marxists view postmodernism as a new strategy to allow the masses cultural expression without serving their real, material interests. Hence, the shifting late-capitalist global decentred configurations of exploitation are actually supported by postmodern superstructural ideological and textual decentring strategies. These level and mix

demanded by the type of stream-of-consciousness film he tries to develop and asks Donald to rescue his script. Once he asks his brother to help him and Donald starts taking things into his perspective, the film itself turns into an action film filled with drugs, chases and murders. Hence, *Adaptation* is not only split into two protagonists but also into two respective thematic and stylistic developments. However, when the film shifts from Charlie's stream-of-consciousness film to his brother's action film the spectator is pulled out of the involvement he had when following the former and pushed towards the latter, which starts suddenly without serious earlier development and out of materials that have been differently contextualized. This perspective shift and narrative split relativizes and neutralizes both world-views. In such ways, postmodern films level and neutralize different positions, rendering the socially potent ones as yet another unprivileged position.

various positions, whereby the potent ones appear as yet another unprivileged position among others, all being apparently *even*.

The revitalization and globalization of the capitalist mode of production in a time of postmodern cultural decentring has posed a dilemma for First World post-Marxists such as Fredric Jameson and David Harvey.[38] They understood the postmodern text – a *simulacrum* or copy devoid of origin yet perceived as real, or a *pastiche* of styles and periods – to be an index of globalizing capitalism. In Harvey's view, late capitalism's mode of 'flexible accumulation', in which shifting flows of capital cross the globe irrespective of national boundaries, often leading to stock market crises and the sudden collapse of Third World economies, translates on the level of cultural production into an unprecedented mutability of the cultural text. According to Jameson, the relentless expansion of globalizing capitalism leads to a reification of human aesthetic and emotive faculties that earlier still resisted capitalist reification. Moreover, the postmodern deconstruction of the imaginary ideal subject (presumed by Althusser and Baudry to hasten the crumbling of the ideological apparatus's blocking of a revolutionary mentality) leads to people's loss of identity, direction, and to their experiencing life through reified disjointed moments. Lost in the postmodern 'schizophrenic' maze, humans fail to cohere time, space and identity, experiencing the non-cohering moments of their lives as a series of temporary and shallow spectacles. Desires and memories are experienced as intense reified sensual excitements or as exchangeable objects that can be bought and sold. These processes are expressed in nostalgic films alluding to an intangible past,[39] in dazzling cinematic spectacles lacking depth or logic, or in television where advertising structures an endless flow of images. Hence, Jameson called for a cognitive remapping of the social, economic, political and cultural terrains through the reconstitution of disparate segments into a continuous act of narration, conceived of as historical revision and future redirection, helping people to reorient themselves in the global maze where they aimlessly move around.

Postcolonial Segmentation in Neshat's *Fervor*

In her split-into-two-screens film *Fervor* (2000), Neshat offers variations upon a constantly frustrated mutual blind desire between a man and a woman, who do not seem to have seen or known each other and yet long for each other's felt presence. In one scene, for example, we see on each screen only one of the protagonists as they each look, or rather blindly search, in the direction of the other in their respective screen. In another sequence they are seen, each alone on a different screen and from respectively opposing points

In face of the First World postmodern co-option of dialectic montage and text-ual disjunction, Jameson seems to turn his back on these textual strategies. Unlike him, however, postcolonial theorists like Hommi Bhabha embrace postmodernism as a subversive strategy for Third world cultural production. Bhabha's postmodern/postcolonial notion of the *mimicry* of First World discourses performed by Third World people, as well as the latter's constant 'in-between' situation stemming from their colonially determined hybrid and split identities, were perceived as destabilizing subversive strategies that constantly dismantle First World attempts to consolidate the ideologies supporting the global configurations of power.[40] Thus, in Bhabha's view, postmodernism is not the dominant ideology of globalizing capitalism as post-Marxists like Jameson think, but rather the expression of its constant destabilization by the hybridity built into the postcolonial situation.

A most interesting articulation of such postmodern/postcolonial destabilizing and unsettling subversion can be found in the work of Iranian-born American artist Shirin Neshat. While her work does not target the First World but rather fundamentalist Iran, her hybrid strategies are exemplary. Hence, in a 1996 untitled photograph we see the fingers of a hand tattooed with Koranic inscriptions silencing the lips of a woman, while at the same the gesture implies that the fingers are being kissed by the lips. The photograph's troubling ambivalence of sensuality and sacredness with no apparent resolution conveys a sense of an impending implosion.

Another disruption of power configurations in a postcolonial film can be seen in Ilia Suleiman's *Divine Intervention* (2002). The film, which tells the story of the insurmountable difficulties faced by a Palestinian couple divided by the Israeli occupation, resorts to ironic fantasies of potency that presumably disrupt the power of the Israeli occupying army. Thus, one scene shows a balloon on which Arafat's face is imprinted floating over an Israeli roadblock, leading the confused and fearful Israeli soldiers to shoot at it ineffectively. In another scene, a Ninja-looking Palestinian confronted by Israeli soldiers suddenly leaps high in the air, swirls and,

---

of view, as they walk towards each other along the same road. However, they do not meet upon arriving in their respective screens at the presumed place of their encounter, as would have happened if they had been seen together on one screen. Hence Neshat, through split-screen strategies that emblematize postcolonial/postmodern segmentation, comments on frustrated desires in fundamentalist, gender-segregated Iran. Her split-screen film revolves around the entangled dialectic of desire and political repression.

as he evades the bullets coming from the amazed soldiers' pistols, he kills them one after the other.

It is arguable whether postcolonial theories and films offer effective postmodern subversions of the First World configurations of power. It is also questionable whether Jameson's suggestion to resort to what amounts to a traditional continuous reorienting narration has any revolutionary import. It may well be that the co-option of dialectic montage and formal disjunction by the postmodern dominant cultural production of the First World is an index of the crumbling of Marxism, while its postmodern appropriation by postcolonialists indicates the impotence of the Third World in the face of globalizing capitalism. On the other hand, in Marxist terms, the spread of postmodernism as the superstructural expression of the process of capitalist globalization may signal the approach of the communist world revolution envisaged by Marx. As Marx predicted, world revolution will come about only after (and because of) the globalization of the capitalist mode of production.

Chapter Summary

Marxism

- Dialectic materialism encapsulates the Marxist conception of natural and human essence as material rather than spiritual and their change as dialectical (i.e. a thesis collides with an antithesis resulting in a synthesis).
- Historical materialism is the Marxist analysis of the evolution of human society according to the method of dialectic materialism.

Marxist Film Constructivism

- The concept of *dialectic film montage* was coined by Soviet avant-garde Marxist *constructivist* filmmakers of the 1920s as an *ideological* film device. It draws upon the Marxist idea of dialectic materialism and concerns an arrangement of film shots in contrasting rather than in complementing or continuous forms, so as to shake or shock rather than appease the spectator.
- The basic idea informing Eisenstein was conflict on all levels of shots and shot editing (thematic, graphic, etc.).
- Vertov insisted on the exclusive use of documentary shots. The Marxist truth could be brought out through the film editor's discovery of the dialectical rhythmic 'interval' in shot juxtapositions.

Deconstructive Neo-Marxism and Film

■ Neo-Marxist film *deconstruction* was based on the use of dialectic montage strategies to lay bare and subvert the dominant capitalist ideological manipulations of the film medium.

■ According to Benjamin, in the age of mechanical reproduction the 'aura' of art collapses. Fascism forces the film medium to offer a fake beautification of film stars and leaders while hiding their brutal politics. Revolutionary filmmakers should use the film to enhance awareness.

■ Althusser argued that ideology twists the relation individuals have to their real conditions of existence, persuading them that they have chosen to be where they were in fact placed.

■ Baudry searched for the 'Ideological Effects of the Basic Cinematographic Apparatus' and found these in the viewing situation; the cine-camera lenses; the film strip; and the continuous editing style. Like Godard in his film, Baudry suggested deconstructing the films' illusion of continuity, centredness and coherence by the use of non-continuous and disjointing dialectic montage strategies.

Anti-colonialist Filmmakers

■ Influenced by Fanon's theses, anti-colonialist filmmakers suggested that films should find ways to better communicate with the Third World exploited masses and incite them to revolution.

Postmodernism, Post-Marxism and Postcolonialism

■ The attributes of the postmodern text — segmentation, character split, spatial and temporal decentring — became the dominant trend in First World capitalist cultural production.

■ For Jameson, the postmodern deconstruction of the centred subject does not lead to revolution as earlier maintained, but leads to people's loss of identity and direction.

■ For postcolonial theorists like Bhabha postmodernist notions of *mimicry* and hybridity are subversive strategies that dismantle First World attempts at consolidating its ideologies.

4 IMAGINARY SIGNIFIERS/ VOYEURISTIC PLEASURES

INTRODUCTION

The psychological effects of films on spectators have intrigued theoreticians since the medium's inception. Two major psychological approaches to film can be discerned. One focuses upon the *conscious* perceptual and cognitive processes through which films are made and comprehended by viewers. Hugo Munstenberg, one of Gestalt psychology's early forerunners, already in 1916 described film as the *art of subjectivity*. In his view, rather than merely copying reality, film aesthetically projects a reality forged according to psychological processes of perception, attention, memory and imagination. Gestalt psychologist Rudolph Arnheim continued this trend, basing his film theory upon the human striving to make film's partial formal configurations cohere through perceptual principles of simplicity, harmony and regularity.[1] More recent cognitivist film theories (see Chapter 2) followed this trajectory, focusing upon how consciously active and coherence-striving viewers construct the story and world of a film flowing in front of them.[2]

Alongside this trajectory another evolved, largely focusing upon the *unconscious* effects that moving images have on the human psyche, particularly upon human emotions. Hence, as discussed in Chapter 1, Jean Epstein developed an associational theory of emotions, according to which moving images are tightly connected to emotions, which in turn offer humans an intuitive and unmediated knowledge of the world, as opposed to the knowledge achieved through rational processes of cognition. Film was for him a psychological apparatus.[3] Sergei Eisenstein also considered film images to evoke unconscious primordial pre-linguistic thoughts and feelings in viewers. Based upon Pavlov's materialist psychology, according to which human behaviour is a result of conditioned reflexes, he believed that films, given the primordial effects of moving images, can powerfully condition spectators through the *shock* instigated by dialectic montage (see Chapter 3). This latter approach, implying powerful unconscious and emotional manipulations of viewers because of the peculiar nature of moving film images, was further developed as we have seen by Althusserian-oriented neo-Marxists. They based their understanding of the *ideological* effects of dominant continuity editing films upon psychoanalytic theses concerning the *psychic* manipulations conducted by such films upon viewers. The psychoanalytic portion of what came to be termed the Althusserian–Lacanian paradigm in film studies is the concern of the first half of this chapter. It deals with the psychic lures and manipulations of film's imaginary signifiers.

The concept of *imaginary signifiers*, a term coined by Christian Metz, brings together the semiotic aspect of film and the psychological effects generated by its unique evocative images and narrative deployment. While following his earlier Saussurean-inspired semiological approach to film (see Chapter 2), Metz shifted his focus of attention to study the psychological effects of film's unique moving images or imaginary signifiers. He enquired how films lure spectators; how films evoke, regulate or channel unconscious desires, notions of identity and the spectators' identification with the film's protagonists.

Metz and others noticed the affinities between moving images projected upon a screen, the reflection of mirrors and the inner means of representation in dreams.[4] In film, mirror and dream, reflections of things perceived as tangible but lacking materiality appear before our eyes or are projected[5] in our minds. Moreover, it seemed that the film spectators' watching conditions – sitting immobile in a darkened theatre, isolated from their surroundings, stimulated only in sight and hearing by the film's flowing images and sounds – encourages in them a hypnotic state.

Psychoanalysis, a discipline that extensively studied dreams as key to the human unconscious and the psychological effects of mirrors on identity formation, was taken to explain these film-viewing processes. Sigmund Freud's *The Interpretation of Dreams*[6] and Jacques Lacan's 'The Mirror Stage as Formative of the Function of the I as Revealed in Psychoanalytic Experience'[7] were two psychoanalytic studies that particularly influenced researchers studying these aspects of film.

I PSYCHOANALYSIS AND FILM

1.1 FREUD'S DREAM WORK

In *The Interpretation of Dreams* Freud rejected previous attempts at explaining dreams as future premonitions, vague and inconsequential residues of daily experiences, or symptoms of bodily sensations. According to Freud, dreams were the key to deciphering the dreamer's psyche since they resulted from the interrelation between conscious and unconscious processes. He viewed conscious processes as the inhibition, elaboration and displacement of desires, impulses, instincts and wishes stemming from an inaccessible unconscious, and their channelling towards venues that allow individuals to lead social lives and face daily reality.

Without such conscious elaboration he maintained, societal and individual life may be threatened by the raw energetic impulses, instincts and wishes stemming from the unconscious. Freud claimed that there was often a disproportion between unconscious impulses and their conscious elaboration, leading to the repression of such impulses and the individual's consequent need to discharge these. He considered slips of the tongue and other mental disruptions of daily life as evidence of the need of repressed impulses to break loose from conscious barriers. Hence, Freud maintained that dreams were one of the major means by which individuals can relieve themselves of these repressed impulses and wishes without threatening their well-being and their mental equilibrium. Therefore, Freud considered the interpretation of dreams to be the key to the unconscious impulses and desires threatening an individual's mental well-being. The need for interpretation stemmed from the fact that the dream's images and voices were scrambled enigmatic manifestations of *latent dream thoughts* through which these repressed impulses and wishes expressed themselves. Dreams were like that because they resulted from an internal mental tension between the individuals' need to relieve the repressed impulses as far as possible and their need to maintain mental equilibrium. Although, when dreaming, individuals are immobilized and allow themselves to experience events that due to their unreality cannot endanger them, a censorship mechanism is nevertheless instituted to prevent the uninhibited impulses from threatening mental equilibrium: 'dreams are given their shape in individual human beings by the operation of two psychical forces...; one of these forces constructs the wish which is expressed by the dream, while the other exercises a censorship upon this dream-wish and, by the use of that censorship, forcibly brings about a distortion in the expression of the wish.'[8]

Freud maintained that the *dream work* (as he termed the process leading to the dream's enigmatic appearance at awakening) consists of four main psychic procedures by which dreamers manage to discharge their repressed impulses and hidden wishes without destabilizing their mental equilibrium: *condensation, displacement, symbolization* and *secondary elaboration*.[9]

Condensation allows the dreamer to cram into few complex images several latent dream thoughts. Freud claimed that evidence of this procedure can be found in those images remembered by the dreamer that are vague or sensed as evading identification. Condensation proceeds by joining together recurring components found in different dream thoughts. It forges new entities composed of different people or complex structures condensed by the imposition of a common denominator.[10] He claimed that the psychoanalyst strives in such cases to unpack the condensed image into its different dream thoughts such as the figuration within a condensed image of the dreamer or someone who threatens him/her.

Displacement procedures aim at shifting the dreamer's attention away from threatening impulses and wishes towards secondary and inconsequential images. Hence, when the dreamer distinctly remembers a certain image, Freud suspects that this distinctness may be evidence of a process of displacement, leading him to search for that which has been obscured by that which appears distinct. For instance, if I remember from my dream the image of a beautiful woman I sat next to on bus number 3, Freud might focus upon the bus number rather than upon the distinct image of the girl.

Symbolization in dreams is also a way to express impulses and concealed wishes. Freud cautions against simplistic interpretations of symbols and the inclination to build a dream-symbol dictionary, since the same symbol can mean different things in an individual's different dreams or for different dreamers. Nevertheless Freud identifies recurrent meanings in the same symbols:

> The Emperor and Empress (or the King and Queen) as a rule really represent the dreamer's parents; and a Prince or Princess represents the dreamer himself or herself ... – all elongated objects, such as sticks, tree trunks and umbrellas (the opening of these last being comparable to an erection) may stand for the male organ ... – as well as all long, sharp weapons, such as knives, daggers and pikes ... – Boxes, cases, chests, cupboards and ovens represent the uterus, and also hollow objects, ships, and vessels of all kinds. – Rooms in dreams are usually women.[11]

Secondary Elaboration consists of an attempt on the part of censorship at re-configuring the dream components into a causal chain within an ordered forward-moving story. This procedure, characterizing conscious operational modes conducted while awake, is imposed upon the dream matter near the moment of awakening from the dream and it is also dominant in daydreams. Secondary elaboration also appears in the midst of dreams, for example, when dreamers, faced with a threatening thought tell themselves, *without waking up*, that 'it is only a dream'. The secondary elaboration is intended to shift the dreamer's attention from the depth axis leading from different manifest dream materials to their underlying dream thoughts, towards a causal developmental axis that leads the dreamer to ascribe meanings that are 'as far removed as possible from their true significance'.[12]

1.2 FILM AS DREAM

Film researchers, particularly during the 1960s, tried to transpose Freud's under-standing of dreams and dream processes to their research on the processes undergone by a viewer when watching a film. They legitimized this transposition by noting the similarity between film's *imaginary signifiers* and dream signifiers, and the similarities in the physical position of film viewer and dreamer. They maintained that in both cases dreamers and viewers are in a state of psychic *regression*, as Freud termed the return and rehearsal by humans of deeper and earlier psychic stages.[13] According to Freud, regression is enabled in dreams because of the loosening of censorship, mainly due to the dreamer's motor paralysis during sleep.[14] This allows dreamers to entertain forbidden thoughts as real yet unthreatening, since imaginary. Likewise, film viewers sit immobile in a darkened space, exposed to tangible yet imaginary events that cannot hurt them. These similarities led film researchers to consider the resemblances between the dream and the film's psychic functions and modes of articulation. While warning that films are not dreams, they nevertheless proposed that viewers and dreamers enter similar mental states. Hence, film viewers also lessen censorship and allow themselves to raise concealed wishes and regress to earlier psychic states. In this sense, films, while external to the viewer, allow viewers to *cathect*[15] their hidden thoughts with the film images and sounds and safely discharge their unconscious impulses and hidden wishes. This may explain the vast amount of sexual and violent imagery pervading films, which according to Freud are the main contents of hidden wishes. It may also explain attempts at film censorship in its affinities to psychic censorship.[16]

Beyond such generalized similarities, film researchers focused upon the relation between dream procedures and film articulation. Hence, attempts were made to decipher symbolization in films according to Freud's interpretations, such as viewing the pistol in the western as a phallic symbol. Likewise displacement was compared to editing transitions between shots or to change of emphasis within a shot (e.g. through shift of focus), while condensation was compared to film dissolves and superimpositions. These resemblances in devices of articulation found application, for example, in attempts made at viewing opening or key film scenes as condensed dreams that the rest of the film unpacks.

Beyond these secondary technical similarities (as Metz called them), which relate to conventional modes of audiovisual articulations shared by both film and dream, Metz spoke of primary similar psychic functions. Hence,

> The device [of lap-dissolve] doesn't simply plot out some relationship between two segments ... it combines their signifiers physically, exactly as in the Freudian definition of the 'means of representation' which characterize dreams... Thus it suggests to us a kind of relationship ... which has to do with the fusion of elements, magical transmutation, mystical efficacy (= the all-powerfulness of thought).[17]

Hence, Metz referred to the psychical function of the film equivalents to 'displacements' and 'condensations' as imparting a feeling of potency to the spectator in their bypassing logical, temporal and spatial constraints. The effects of the film's imposition of such magical elasticity upon the figured reality is not unlike Freud's claim that dreams often express the dreamer's concealed infantile wish to overcome reality constraints. Similar psychic functions can be found in the tendency of classical films to cut or move the camera away from a violent or sexually disturbing event towards a 'safe' place, such as when moving the camera away from figuring a sexual intercourse to a lit fireplace, or when tilting up the camera away from the figuration of a violent murder towards the sky.

Metz found Freud's notion of secondary elaboration to be the dominant aspect shared by film and dream, which also clarified the difference between the two. According to Metz, the film's narrative is closer to the functioning of secondary elaboration in daydreams. Freud positioned daydreams between dreaming and being awake, differentiating daydreams from dreams by the saliency of secondary elaboration in the former and by its reversed functioning. Hence, while in dreams secondary elaborations aim at diverting the dreamer's attention away from the relation between dream material and dream thoughts by imposing a causal narrative upon the dream segments, in daydreams their function is to *insulate* the partly awake individual from external reality. Thus, *through* an apparently logical, flowing and continuous narrative, daydreamers enter a dreamy state allowing them the discharging of unconscious impulses. According to Metz, film narratives function like secondary elaborations in daydreams. They immerse viewers into films through their flowing narratives. The film's imposition of narrative upon its images and sounds allows viewers to discharge their repressed impulses and wishes through the images and sounds of the film. The film viewer enters *through* the narrative into the semi-conscious situation characterizing the daydreamer.

Film as Dream: *An Andalusian Dog*

The affinities between film and dream have led many filmmakers to include within their films dream sequences or construct their film as dream. Buñuel's and Dali's surrealist film *An Andalusian Dog* is consciously informed by Freud's dream theory.[18] The film includes powerful symbols such as ants crawling out of the palm of a hand; condensations such as a complex image of the film's protagonist attempting to drag a grand piano with two dead bleeding donkeys on top and two live priests tied to the back; displacements such as the cut from a blade about to slash a woman's eyeball to an analogous crossing of a bright moon by a blade-shaped dark cloud (but Buñuel and Dali nevertheless return in a shocking shot to the eyeball being slashed). The film however,

1.3 LACAN'S MIRROR STAGE

In 'The Mirror Stage as Formative of the Function of the I', the psychoanalyst Lacan introduced the hypothesis that our first notion of identity, occurring between the ages of six and eighteen months, is based upon a mere reflection of ourselves. This self-reflection, either in mirrors or by deduction from seeing our kind through a highly developed sense of sight, appears coherent, whole and continuous. It counters our inner sensation of being disjointed and incoherent due to our undeveloped motor coordination: 'The fact is that the total form of the body by which the subject anticipates in a mirage the maturation of his power is given to him only as *Gestalt*, that is to say, in an exteriority in which this form is certainly more constituent than constituted.'[20] Important for Lacan was that this intangible homogeneous reflection positions the 'I [ego] in a fictional direction, which will always remain irreducible for the individual'.[21] This reflection, responsible for our initial sense of self, also introduces an insurmountable lack between its full homogeneous appearance and our inner sense of self, a lack we will futilely strive to fill throughout our lives.[22] Lacan likened this initial sense of selfhood to Freud's Ideal ego.[23] in the sense that we strive to identify with this self-image, a striving also informing our secondary identification with others. This process of identification should be understood as 'the transformation that takes place in the subject when he assumes an image'.[24]

According to Lacan, this initial reflection-induced sense of self occurs at the intersection between two cardinal modes of cognition. He hypothesized that before the mirror stage humans perceive their surroundings within what he called the *imaginary* mode of cognition, in which there is no apprehension of a difference between an inside and an outside (perceived as continuous and undifferentiated much like the way the world appears through our sense of sight). This corresponds

---

neutralizes Freud's concept of secondary elaboration in that narrative connections between the film segments are disjointed. In that, as Metz would have it, the film, despite its powerful and fascinating images reveals the difference between film and dream. This is because its disjointed nature causes the viewer to be aware and interpretative rather than enter a dreamy atmosphere. According to Metz then, the common narrative film better induces in viewers the semi-conscious mode that immerses them in the film world by using the narrative flow to avoid their conscious mind's wandering away and pondering upon the film's construction.[19]

to Freud's claim that during this stage human infants identify with their mothers on whom they are totally dependent and whom they perceive as an extension of themselves. Lacan hypothesized that it is during the mirror stage that the imaginary order of cognition is overlain by the rise to consciousness of the *symbolic* order, characterized by the ability to perceive discrete units and differentiate between them. The rise to consciousness of the symbolic order, which structures the unconscious like a language according to Lacan, is the basis for the acquisition of language. As he mentions, Freud also detected this transition in the 'Fort-Da!' game played by infants at this stage, where they enjoy the appearance and disappearance of objects, indicating their comprehension of discreteness and difference.[25] The Lacanian symbolic order precedes and is the precondition for the infant's differentiation between male and female during the Oedipal stage.[26]

1.4 FILM AND THE MIRROR STAGE

Several psychoanalytically inclined film researchers presumed that it is possible to derive an understanding of the processes of identification undergone by film viewers from Lacan's mirror-stage theory. They based this on the apparent similarities between film signifiers and the reflection in mirrors; on a certain comparison between the infant's physical condition during the mirror stage and the adult viewer facing a film; and on the notion that the film-viewing situation induces in viewers a regression and rehearsal of earlier psychic stages. Hence, the film viewer sits in a darkened theatre, enhancing eyesight, which is also the most developed sense during the mirror stage. Also, film images flow before the viewer without coordination to the viewer's sitting position, in a way that is reminiscent of the infant's uncoordinated relation to the reflection in the mirror. Finally, the flowing film's imaginary signifiers correspond to the imaginary order of cognition dominant during the mirror stage when infants develop their initial sense of self. Although film is not a mirror, and the viewer, unlike the mirror-stage infant, has a developed sense of identity, the regression induced in the viewer by the film, and the fact that film reflects whatever stood in front of it, left for these researchers reason to presume that the viewer in some way rehearses the mirror-stage experience. What characterizes this experience is a feeling of joy noticed by Lacan each time an infant approached a mirror. Lacan related this joy to the infant's self-perception through its reflection as a coordinated, whole and continuous body. As mentioned, following this initial joy the unbridgeable gap between this full reflected image and the infant's inner feeling develops. Film researchers suggested that one of film's major appeals to viewers stems from their rehearsal of the feeling of joy felt in front of their reflection during the mirror stage, a feeling they long for all their lives. How do films generate such a rehearsal?

The answer provided by film Lacanians derived precisely from the difference between the adult viewer and the mirror-stage infant, as well as from the fact that viewers do not see their *own* reflection in the film. Their claim was that the viewer's first identification is not with the characters or any other objects figured within the film reflections, but rather *with the point of view of the camera.* This identification, of which viewers are usually made unaware, enables the reinforcement of their sense of identity because it gives them an illusion that *they* originate the images flowing before their eyes, and that without their presence these images would lack the fullness and continuity characterizing them. They argued that this stems from the structure of the camera lenses and from other devices that create most films' continuous three-dimensional imaginary flow. As noticed already,[27] the camera creates a centred space converging into the viewer's eye whereby there occurs a simultaneous centring of space and viewer. According to these theorists, this dual centring is responsible for the viewers' self-perception as origin of the film so long as viewers are not consciously aware of the camera's presence. Therefore, for instance, the dominant fiction-film rule that the film protagonists never look into the camera lenses (for otherwise the viewers' identification with the camera's point of view may collapse). Moreover, they argued that camera movements and the seamless continuity editing of shots further reinforce the viewers' sense of omnipotence over a flowing reality 'made' by them and designed for them.

These premises served as the basis for many variations on the identification processes undergone by film viewers. Metz, for instance, studied the film's inducement of the mirror stage in viewers and its effects upon their positioning as peeping Toms in dominant continuity-styled filmmaking.[28] He maintained that spectators are positioned as peeping Toms or voyeurs by films where actors behave as if nobody is watching them. Although in theatre the same rule usually applies, an exhibitionist component is always present in the live encounter of actor and spectator, so that both parties are aware of each other's presence. In film, however, the exhibitionism present in theatre is lacking since the spectator peeps upon a world that is visually tangible but which he knows is absent. This peeping Tom, with no fear of getting caught, who identifies with the camera's point of view and who is immersed in the fictional reality of the film, loses his self-awareness as a separate entity since:

> That which is seen does not know that it is seen … and its lack of awareness allows the voyeur to be himself unaware that he is a voyeur. All that remains is the brute fact of seeing: the seeing of an outlaw, of an *Id* unrelated to any *Ego*, a seeing which has no features or position, as vicarious as the narrator-God or the spectator-God.[29]

Hence, in Metz's variation, the viewers' identification with the camera does not empower their sense of self as different from the film, but rather reinforces their *imaginary* mode of cognition in which their point of view, which is that of the camera, is an omnipotent transcendental entity projecting the film's flowing images.

Daniel Dayan offered another variation on the mirror-stage resonances in film viewers.[30] He was concerned with the effects of continuity editing on the viewer. In his view, continuity editing transitions, particularly in shot–reverse-shot constructs, are based on the *suturing* of the viewer's consciousness into the film. Shot–reverse-shot constructs consist of a sequence of shots in which the viewer watches character B from the point of view of character A, followed by a shot showing the reverse angle in which A is seen from B's point of view (and so on). Dayan claimed that in the first shot (showing character B) the spectators fully identify with the camera's point of view and sense themselves as originating the image. However, in the transition to the reverse shot the imaginary continuity may be broken due to the change in camera angle and figuration, potentially raising in the viewers' minds the question of who is showing them the event, a question threatening to lay bare the film apparatus and destroy the illusion and the spectators' attendant joyful empowerment. However, according to Dayan, the shot–reverse-shot construct manipulates the potential raising of such a question to serve its needs. This is because the reverse shot offers a retroactive answer to the viewer's question, whereby it was character A that *was* watching character B. Thus the film diverts the answer to the viewer's question from the level of the film apparatus (i.e. the question raises the awareness to how the film is made), to the fictional level suggesting something like 'it was the character that you see now that was watching the character you just saw'. Through such manipulations (termed by Dayan 'the tutor code of cinema'), viewers' minds are sutured into the film and their illusionary empowerment is not only reinstated but reinforced.[31]

The Lacanian-derived ideas on the visual imaginary of film were also extended to the rather neglected auditory film channel. Altman, for instance, raised the possibility that film sound may affect spectators the way Lacanians presumed film images affected them: 'Even the Greeks, however, knew that the story of Narcissus is incomplete without that of Echo.'[32] The audio mirror completes the video mirror.'[33] Mary Ann Doane also elaborated upon this notion of sound in film, claiming that it enhances the viewer's immersion. She argued that the subjection of sound to image in the dominant continuity edited film illusorily enlarges the visual space beyond the rectangular screen into the theatre, engulfing the spectator. The multidirectional spreading of sound along with the imaginary effects of the visual track enhances the film's mirror-stage effects upon spectators.

1.5 CRITIQUES OF THE ANALOGIES 'FILM AS DREAM' AND 'FILM AS MIRROR'

Notwithstanding the evocative comparisons of films to dreams or mirrors there seems to be a 'suturing' of the striking differences between these,[34] particularly of the fact that film is a conscious activity, external to the viewer and probably consumed consciously. Cognitivists in particular attacked this psychoanalytic approach to film. Carroll tried to dismantle one after another the key concepts used in such theories.[35] For instance, he rejected the idea concerning the viewer's identification with the camera or with protagonists in the film. What identification basically implies, contended Carroll, is that individuals are made to think that they are the camera or the protagonist and are therefore immersed in the film or think they author it. Considering these ideas far-fetched, Carroll proposed that viewers can get involved with a film or its protagonists by presuming the films to offer '*if this was to happen*' type propositions. Likewise, Carroll claimed that the difference between films and dreams is greater than their similarity. For example, he rejected the presumed similarity of dream motor paralysis with the immobility of film viewers on the verifiable ground that spectators, unlike dreamers, can look back towards the projector at any moment. Furthermore, if viewers are late, they can slowly walk to their seats *while* watching the movie, and can even get up and touch the screen in case they have doubts about whether what they are watching is not there. He also rejected the notion of film *suture* on the grounds that it presupposes a far-fetched process whereby the viewer undergoes several different consecutive mental states (I think I am the origin of the image, then I think for a moment that I am not, then I think again that I am the origin since I concluded that the character, rather than anyone else, is watching the shot I am seeing now). Cognitivists in general rejected psychoanalytic approaches to films because of their bypassing of the viewers' conscious activities.

The semiotic–psychoanalytic approach to processes of identification in films was also attacked by feminist and queer film theorists. While they espoused many of the teachings of psychoanalysis (and neo-Marxism), they claimed that semiotic psychoanalysts failed to address the different effects that imaginary signifiers have on different spectators. They also suspected that the positioning of a generalized non-gendered spectator, even though often articulated from a neo-Marxist critical perspective, ultimately conformed to a white-male-heterosexual dominated social order. Films, they claimed, are perceived differently by, and differently affect different people.

2 VARYING VOYEURISTIC PLEASURES

Feminists, post-feminists and queer theorists strove to fill the major omissions implied in the Althusserian–Lacanian positioning of a generalized subject by studying the voyeuristic pleasures and displeasures offered by films to both genders (feminists) or to non-heterosexuals (queer theorists). Nevertheless, 1980s' feminists, while exchanging capitalism and class struggle for patriarchy and the repression of women, tended to accept the Althusserian–Lacanian conception of the dominant continuity edited film as psychic-ideological manipulation and its deconstruction as an effective strategy to open the medium to the concerns of women. Post-feminists and queer theorists of the 1990s, on the other hand, attacked deconstructive feminism for its dead-end conception of film deconstruction and its binary conception of gender that neglected non-heterosexual sensibilities. They offered instead a poststructural conception of gender as a fluid rather than a fixed identity, focusing on how spectators bend any film, whether continuous or not, to serve their unstable and shifting identities.

2.1 FEMINIST DECONSTRUCTION OF FILM'S (MALE) VOYEURISTIC PLEASURES

The term feminism, denoting women's social struggle surfaced by the end of the nineteenth century and gained currency through the writings of Virginia Woolf and Simone de Beauvoir. In the 1960s feminism became widespread as the social struggle for women rights and their emancipation, particularly in the USA, as part of the wider student revolution and the struggle for human rights. According to feminist historians, 1960s' feminism was *essentialist* and largely derived the differences between the sexes from biological differences. It claimed that in patriarchal societies the female essence is repressed. This repressed essence, characterized as receptive, passive, altruist, and striving for social equality and solidarity was opposed to a dominant male essence characterized by invasiveness, aggressiveness, competitiveness, egocentricity and individualism. Different feminist positions strove during the 1960s and early 1970s to find ways in which the female essence might better society. Thus liberal feminism joined the ranks of the human rights movement so as to better the situation of women as a repressed minority, to give women freedom of expression and to equalize their status with that of men in the workplace and in government. Marxist-oriented feminists defined the ideas of equality and solidarity as essentially female and capitalism as essentially male. They tried to overlap gender and class struggles, claiming that women, although spread across different social classes, form an exploited group within each class. Radical feminists, on the other hand, influenced by hippie culture, tried to develop alternative ways of life such as female communities organized around the values stemming from the female essence. While these early essentialist feminist positions lacked a serious film approach and focused on content analysis of gender representations, the mid-1970s' emergence of a deconstructive anti-essentialist feminism, in its focus upon cultural constructs, generated an interesting body of film theory.

Deconstructive anti-essentialist feminism evolved from a criticism of the 1960s' feminist biological determinism and essentialism. Rather than basing gender differences upon biology, deconstructive feminists conceived the differences between the sexes and the characteristics ascribed to each as institutionalized and structured by culture, particularly by language and other forms of communication. This approach led them to lay bare and deconstruct the cultural structuring of gender, presuming that this would lead to new conceptions of gender and to a re-evaluation and redefinition of ascribed values and functions. Psychoanalysis, conceived of as a theory stemming from patriarchy and focused on human sexuality, was taken to reveal the 'patriarchal unconscious' conception of women that informed the dominant cultural constructs discriminating against women and promoting their subjugation.

Laura Mulvey's groundbreaking article 'Visual Pleasure and Narrative Cinema'[36] introduced a gendered split in the generalized spectator assumed by the Althusserian–Lacanian paradigm. Mulvey's major presumption was that films were a product of the 'patriarchal unconscious' and therefore served the patriarchal social order by replicating and reinforcing gender patterns that discriminated against women. Psycho-analysis, which she considered to reveal the patriarchal unconscious, was particularly apt for laying bare the ways by which films discriminate. Mulvey found the source of this discrimination in Freud's analysis of the Oedipus complex. Freud placed the Oedipal phase during which boys and girls forge a defined sexual identity at the core of the unconscious. Mulvey claimed that Freud's sloppy or partial description of the girl's sexual identity formation and of what Freud termed the 'positive' case of the boy's sexual formation[37] stemmed from Freud's own patriarchal unconscious and revealed the source of discrimination of women in patriarchal society.

According to Freud, during the pre-Oedipal stage human infants feel fulfilled: the mother takes care of all their needs and is perceived by infants as their extension. This stage, as mentioned in the preceding section, conforms to Lacan's imaginary order of cognition. At a certain point, claimed Freud, the infant realizes that his/her mother is not always present to cater to her/his needs. This enrages and frustrates her/him. The conclusion the infant reaches is that the reason for the mother's absence is the father, a conclusion leading him/her to want to get rid of the father so as to reunite with the mother. Freud even presumed that the primeval father was actually murdered by his sons. The desire to get rid of the father engenders in the infant a great fear from what the father might do to him/her for entertaining such thoughts. The infant finds the answer to what the father might do in the biological difference between male and female. (According to Freud, the realization of a difference between the sexes introduces the infant into language, which is based on the ability to conduct binary distinctions. Lacan termed this the *symbolic order* of cognition, which he claimed originated during the 'mirror stage' that pre-dates the Oedipus complex.) According to Freud, the infant interprets the difference between the sexes as a *lack* of penis in the mother. This leads to the perception of the mother as someone who has already been punished for a sin she committed in the past. Henceforth, the infant's fear of being castrated by the father, as probably happened to the mother, leads the *boy* to identify with the authoritative, punitive figure of the father. The *girl*, in a symmetrical inversion, begins to suffer from a *penis envy*. This results in her identification with the mother and her developing an erotic love for the father stemming from her wish to find completion through his penis.

The boy's process of identification out of fear internalizes in the boy's mind the father figure as his superego, representing patriarchal law and ethics. The girl, on the other hand, due to social sanctions, transfers her completion-derived erotic love of the father towards real or symbolic substitutes. Giving birth to a boy and raising him into the patriarchal order is one such symbolic completion.

The Freudian patriarchal analysis of the Oedipus complex has dire consequences for women. According to it, women are perceived as having committed a primal sin evident in their 'bleeding wound', as Freud described it. Woman is also conceived as lacking the ability to fully internalize patriarchal societal ethics and law, relegating her to the function of *non-male*. This conception allows the social construction of the male as bearer of law and meaning, and of woman as bearer of children and their raising into the patriarchal order. Woman remains in man's mind as a memory of pre-Oedipal fullness and hence his desire for her; or as post-Oedipal lack, and hence as symbolizing his fear of castration.

Mulvey, considering films to be a product of the patriarchal unconscious, searched in Freud's interpretation of the Oedipus complex for an explanation of the way films reinforce and spread the patriarchal conception of the genders. She started by asking why people like to watch movies, a question that led her to enquire why people like to watch at all. This is because films, according to Mulvey, cater to people's scopophilia or love of watching. It pleasures the viewer's gaze while channelling it towards its needs. She found in Freud's writings two different sources for scopophilia: erotic and narcissistic scopophilia. While erotic scopophilia stems from sexual desire towards *another*, in narcissistic scopophilia we gaze at others because they are *like* ourselves (narcissistic scopophilia corresponds to Lacan's 'mirror stage' when infants find in the anthropomorphic form of others a reinforcement of their sense of selfhood).

Mulvey found a contradiction between the two types of scopophilia. While erotic scopophilia is based upon a *difference* between the seeing and the seen, the narcissistic gaze looks for *sameness*. According to Mulvey, classical film developed two dominant modes of articulation, each catering to a different scopophilic urge. Hence, in the spectacular portions of film, the human figure is there to be looked at erotically from another's point of view. Spectacle is therefore static, and the human figure is restricted in its spatial movement, usually seen within a flattened image. The directionally evolving narrative, on the other hand, caters to our narcissistic urge. It revolves around a figure with which viewers identify. This identification is achieved by correlating the viewer's point of view with that of a character who is placed at the centre of a three-dimensional space that it controls and whose actions drive the narrative development. The viewers' sense of self is reinforced through the identification of their point of view with that of this 'larger than life' protagonist (who nevertheless resembles the viewer).

Mulvey pointed out that since classical films express the patriarchal unconscious, women usually figure in the spectacular portion of films while men control the film's narrative space. Hence women are positioned as erotic objects for the viewer's gaze, lacking their own point of view and figured in an enclosed or flattened space which they inhabit passively and statically. Men, on the other hand, are there to be identified with. Through their point of view the viewer watches how they change the course of events while dynamically moving within their controlled three-dimensional narrative space. Often, said Mulvey, a tension develops between the two-dimensional static space of spectacle and the three-dimensional dynamic narrative space. One of film's major strategies to overcome this spatial tension is through the overlap of the viewer's and the male hero's points of view upon the spectacle and the woman figured within it. Thus woman is figured as an erotic object for both the male protagonist and the viewer. According to Mulvey, these modes of articulation reproduce and reinforce the gender figurations and functions ascribed by patriarchal society.

Mulvey then turned to Freud's contention that woman symbolizes for the male, in her sexual presence, his fear of castration. Filmmakers, claimed Mulvey, found ways to neutralize this fear within each mode of articulation. Hence, in the spectacle mode, catering to erotic scopophilia, the neutralization of the fear of castration is achieved by the fetishization of the woman's figure. According to Freud, fetishism is a process whereby the desire for the forbidden and threatening sexual organ is transferred to substitutes. For instance, instead of raising the gaze towards the forbidden and threatening sex organ, the gaze is fixated upon the shoe, which becomes the desired fetish. Mulvey found in Von Sternberg's spectacle-dominated films a fetishization of the figure of Marlene Dietrich (e.g. *Morocco*, 1930). Not only did he obsessively shoot Dietrich from overlapping angles and within static situations on account of narrative development, but he used different filters or cloths over the camera lenses, as well as disjointing her body through close-ups of her different body parts, thereby attempting to neutralize her threatening sexuality. Thus, concluded Mulvey, Sternberg exchanged Dietrich's threatening sexual presence for an exalted, lofty fetishized beauty, and fetishized parts of her body by disjointing her full image.

While Von Sternberg represented for Mulvey the spectacular strategy of fetishization, Hitchcock was taken by her to represent the use of a sadistic strategy in narrative dominated films to neutralize woman's symbolization of the castration threat. Mulvey identified in Hitchcock an erotically driven sadistic attitude towards his female heroines.[38] Hitchcock deals in several of his films with a male protagonist who is on the side of the law, who gets into trouble because of a woman suspected of a crime or somehow tied to it. The male hero conducts a sadistic investigation of the woman, aimed at revealing the reasons for the crime she is tied to and save her once he establishes her innocence. Mulvey found Hitchcock's films (e.g. *Rear Window*, 1954 and *Marny*, 1964) to follow a male protagonist who moved in a three-dimensional space and through whose point of view the suspected female was looked at in an erotic/scrutinizing way. She saw in the man's following of the woman and in his investigation/interrogation of her a sadistic process aimed at revealing her primal sin and exposing her innocence or guilt, thus neutralizing the fear of castration she symbolized.

Mulvey's conclusion was that the dominant type of filmmaking (mostly from Hollywood) mainly addressed the male spectator whose scopophilic gaze it pleasured. It allowed him to identify with the male protagonist controlling the narrative and reinforced his sense of identity. It also allowed him to gaze erotically at the female protagonist who inhabited the spectacle portions of the film. Mulvey

---

Fetishism and Sadism in Buñuel's *Belle de jour*

A brief scene from Buñuel's *Belle de jour* aptly illustrates Mulvey's contentions (see p. 56 for a summary of the film's plot). In the scene we are shown an erotic fetishist/sadist interaction between a young and handsome delinquent (Pierre Clémenti) and the film's female protagonist (Catherine Deneuve) whom the young man considers to be a mysterious, beautiful looking whore. From the delinquent's point of view, we see the woman as she lies naked on a bed in the brothel where she works. The handsome young man dressed in black leather stands over her, questioning her about where she lives and what else she does while scrutinizing her perfect-looking body. The castration fear underlining this erotic fetishist/sadist interaction surfaces when the

concluded that female spectators have no real place in the theatre. In order to enjoy the movie, they must adopt the male gaze, which leads them to watch their kind as erotic object. This schizophrenic positioning of women spectators led Mulvey to call for a deconstruction of these patriarchal film constructs. She suggested, for example, deconstructing the conflation of the spectator's, the camera's and the male protagonist's point of view so as to liberate the spectator and the camera from the film's imposition of female discrimination. Nevertheless, Mulvey didn't think such deconstructive strategies could lead to an alternative type of filmmaking, given that patriarchal discrimination against woman is institutionalized in all venues of communication. Therefore she found attempts at inverting the film's positioning of genders to be misleading since, given the larger social patriarchal structure of discrimination, such attempts are perceived as either absurd or as clothing women in man's clothes.[40] A brief look from Mulvey's point of view at films that intend such a strategy of inversion, such as *Silence of the Lambs* or *Thelma and Louise* (1991), reveals that their positioning of women in the centre of the films' narrative trajectory does not lend them the power afforded to similarly positioned men. Hence, the placing of FBI apprentice Clarice Sterling (Judy Foster) at the centre of the narrative in *Silence of the Lambs*, and her apparent control of the narrative through her search for a serial killer of women, results in an asexual character ultimately driven by male characters (Hannibal Lecter, the incarcerated cannibal who guides her through hints to the serial killer and her FBI patronizing boss) and by an uncontrolled psychological urge to quiet the bleating of the lambs pounding in her head since childhood. Likewise, Thelma and Louise, once they kill a guy who has raped one of them and begin their flight from the police, start to shed their initial femininity and gradually intertextually reference two male cowboy outlaws on the run. Their

---

young man commands the woman to turn around. When she does, he suddenly retreats, repelled by a birthmark he sees on her skin. He tells her to get dressed. The 'tainting' of the woman's beautiful perfect fetishized body by a birthmark enhances her sexual presence and his fear of castration. The narcissism involved in this sadistic interaction is made explicit when, as the woman gets dressed and tells the young man she likes him, he arrogantly replies that 'it is normal'. He then smiles at her, revealing he has missing teeth. This offers the final evidence of his castration fear since losing one's teeth is taken by Freud to symbolize castration.[39]

transgendering is reinforced by the traditional figuration of other female characters in the film, and is rejected in their final punishment by the film's narrative that has them both committing suicide. It is this apparent dead-end situation that led Mulvey to reject altogether the dominant type of narrative films, calling for constant deconstruction: 'Women, whose image has continually been stolen and used for this end, cannot view the decline of the traditional film form with anything much more than sentimental regret'.[41]

Mulvey herself, along with Peter Wollen, tried to put her theory into practice in their film *Riddles of the Sphinx* (1977) where they audiovisually investigated and deconstructed the codes of narrative cinema in an attempt to evoke an alternative mode of articulation through which to render female representations in film. Hence, the film breaks the conventional fetishized representation of females by conveying Louise, the film's female protagonist, through fragmented imagery and soundtrack, consisting of multiple female voices and viewpoints. These generated ambiguous meanings that deconstructed stable and accepted figurations and symbolizations of women in film and society.

Mulvey's theory inspired a barrage of feminist film research but also drew criticism. A major criticism was that she did not actually address the female spectator's evident pleasure. Particularly interesting was Gaylin Studlar's suggestion

Masquerading in *Yentl* and *Boys Don't Cry*

The most salient examples of masquerading are evident in films where female actors cross-dress, as in *Yentl* (1983) or in *Boys Don't Cry* (1999). While these films offer different grounds for cross-dressing and belong to different genres, in both clothing masks the shape of the female body, thereby fluctuating between its spectacled eroticization and its narrative agency. These films offer the woman protagonist true agency and point of view, while disjointing the usual conflation of the camera's point of view with that of the male protagonist upon the woman as object of desire. This strategy opens up a space where female spectators can identify with the female protagonist's agency without assuming a male sadist point of view, while also deriving voyeuristic pleasure from watching the male protagonist as object of desire through the point of view of the masked female protagonist. Hence Yentl (Barbra Streisand), who disguises herself as a boy to study the Torah in a yeshiva, a forbidden activity for women in an East European Jewish town at the beginning of the twentieth century, befriends Avigdor (Mandy Patinkin), another student in the yeshiva, on intellectual grounds. This initially deflates their mutual looks from eroticism and later inverts the traditional roles when he is seen erotically from Yentl's point of view. Likewise, in *Boys Don't Cry*, Teena Brandon (Hilary Swank) on the run from the law cross-dresses

that the understanding of the spectators' pleasure be based upon the psychoanalytic concept of masochism as opposed to Mulvey's reliance upon sadism. The
masochistic model 'rejects a stance that has emphasized the phallic phase and the
pleasure of control or mastery and therefore offers an alternative to strict Freudian
models that have proven a dead end for feminist-psychoanalytic theory'.[42] Masochism, claimed Studlar (following Deleuze), originates in the pre-Oedipal stage
and is dominated by the desire to reunite with the mother figure and rehearse the
feeling of plenitude. It seemed, therefore, more apt to deal with the imaginary
plenitude that films articulate. The masochistic model emphasized 'fantasy,
disavowal, fetishism, and suspense',[43] traits that are particularly characteristic
of the genre of melodrama, which is popular with female spectators. However,
while this model elaborated upon masochistically derived pleasures, it ultimately
reinforced Mulvey's claim that female spectators are left to identify themselves with
their being objects of desire.

In a later article, entitled 'Afterthoughts on "Visual Pleasure and Narrative
Cinema" inspired by *Duel in the Sun*',[44] Mulvey herself tried to address the pleasures
of the female spectator. She found in Freud's later writings the contention that
femininity is forged by the repression of male traits present during the pre-Oedipal
stage, mainly the repression in the girl of the perception of the ego as free, superior

---

as Brandon Teena in a Nebraska town, where he/she
hangs out with a group of boys and dates beautiful Lana
(Chloë Sevigny). The film both destabilizes the 'natural'
masculinity of the other boys, whose drinking or cursing
are estranged and assume a degree of playfulness
due to her presence among them, and deflates the
homoeroticism implied in the relationship between
Brandon and Lana due to the discordance between Lana's
traditional femininity and Brandon's 'male' sensitivity.
However, the subversion implied in masquerading often
fails due to its overriding reappropriation into the
common patriarchal representation of woman as object
of desire. This happens in cross-dressing films once the
secret is revealed, leading to a forceful return of the
repressed. Hence, in *Yentl*, it takes the form of enhanced
romanticism and eroticization of the female body, as in
the scene depicting Yentl's love affair with Avigdor once
her secret is revealed. In *Boys Don't Cry*, the revelation
of the secret leads to tragic sadistic consequences for
Teena who is betrayed, humiliated, raped and murdered
by her former buddies. This return of the repressed
creates such emotional luring or distress that the gap
opened by the masquerade is tightly reinstated, leading
female spectators to succumb through their identification
with the female protagonist to a retrogressive position
leaving them again with no options.

and invulnerable. She then concluded that female spectators can identify with the male protagonist in its representing this freedom of the ego, thus unloading their repressed ego freedom. Mulvey rejected of course Freud's unfounded bias in his tagging of traits belonging to the pre-Oedipal stage, when the infant does not feel gendered yet, as male or female. Nevertheless, the reinforcement of the ego fantasy occurs in the adult female spectator out of identification with a male figure, and this generates again a split female spectator.

Other deconstructivist feminists, such as Mary Ann Doane, tried to offer a way out from Mulvey's dead-end by suggesting the notion of *masquerading* as a subversive strategy on the part of women performers and spectators in films: 'Masquerade ... constitutes an acknowledgment that it is femininity itself which is constructed as mask – as the decorative layer which conceals a non-identity.'[45] Moreover, by exaggerating femininity, female spectators can create the critical distance between the figuration of women in patriarchal films and their viewing it. This distance is however lacking for females in non-masqueraded performances or spectatorship because 'For the female spectator there is a certain over-presence of the image – she is the image.'[46] Therefore, according to Doane, female spectators, unless using the masquerading strategy, are left with two choices: 'the masochism of over-identification or the narcissism entailed in becoming one's own object of desire... The affectivity of masquerade lies precisely in its potential to manufacture a distance from the image, to generate a problematic within which the image is manipulable, producible, and readable by the woman.'[47]

Doane's notion of masquerade informed the emergence of post-feminism. Post-feminists criticized deconstructive feminism's dead-end. In line with poststructural and postcolonial positions, post-feminists offered an understanding of femininity as a fluid rather than fixed identity. This opened the way for, or coalesced with, queer theories that addressed a variety of always unstable gay, lesbian, bisexual, transgender and even straight sensibilities.

2.2 POST-FEMINIST AND QUEER THEORIES OF VOYEURISTIC PLEASURES

The poststructural revolution (see Chapter 2) informed the growing criticism of deconstructive feminism. Michel Foucault critiqued psychoanalysis as a widespread discourse on sexuality carried out within social configurations of power and lacking a critique or redefinition of these. He also suggested that such critique and redefinition could and should stem from a discussion of the body and its figuration in different discourses. This inspired post-feminists like Luce Irigaray to look again at the female body in search of the possibility of instituting a different discourse on femininity. Irigaray claimed that women have 'sex organs more or less everywhere'.[48] According to her, the multiple erogenous zones of the female body evoke a plurality of pleasures which are decentred and incoherent. This sexuality is also reflected in a non-male approach to language, a polysemic and shifting relation to it that constantly subverts the patriarchal notion of a stable, centred identity. While uncomfortable with Irigaray's implied essentialism, Doane nevertheless suggested that using the body as clothes-hanger on which the discussion of the relation of the body to processes of signification can be hung allows for the development of a new definition of femininity within the power struggles among discourses on sexuality, without the need to resort to biological essentialism.[49] Irigaray's and Doane's evolving post-feminism shared the poststructural perception of the split subject that replaced the centred structuralist subject.

The post-feminist understanding of femininity as a fluid rather than fixed identity opened the way or coalesced with queer theories that addressed in such manner all sexual and gender identities, particularly those of gays, lesbians, bisexuals and transgendered people. As stated by Doty, 'Queer theory shares with feminism an interest in non-straight normative expressions of gender and with lesbian, gay, and bisexual studies a concern with non-straight expressions of sexuality and gender.'[50] However, queer theory goes beyond these perspectives in that it focuses upon transgressions of established gender or sexual identities, be they straight, gay or lesbian. Hence, rather than presuming a fixed or essentialist stable identity, even if this identity is fixed-as-fluid the way post-feminists often characterized femininity, queer theory presumes all sexual and gender identities to be hybrid and in a potential or actual fluid state.

Queer theory, however, critiqued the long-held binary opposition of male to female identities that still resonated in the writings of post-feminists. They argued that this binary opposition was designed to exclude varied sexual and social subjects assuming gay, lesbian, bisexual and transgender identities, since the latter, when viewed from the point of view of the male/female divide, were considered abnormal digressions.

Judith Butler's *Gender Trouble*[51] expanded the post-feminist position on femininity as diverse, split, shifting and polysemic to characterize all sexual identities. Butler's queer theory argued that not only deconstructive feminism, in its exchange of biological essentialism with a no-less determining binary cultural determinism, but also the post-feminists' return to the body as grounds for grouping women, ultimately led to a dead-end. Feminism was altogether wrong in its presumption that women or men are groups with clear gender attributes. In her mind, biological sexual differences do not determine gender characteristics or imply a desire for the other sex. While 'bodies matter', as she claimed, gender and sexual desire are seen by her as variables that may change in different contexts. She proposed to view gender as something both assigned to and assumed by people, as a *performance* on their part rather than as an inextricably fixed, essential or inescapably culturally determined identity. As she put it: 'There is no gender identity behind the expressions of gender; … identity is performatively constituted by the very "expressions" that are said to be its results.'[52] Moreover, Butler suggested that the dominant binary performance of male/female genders, which relegates to the periphery other performances labelled as *queer*, is a relational configuration of power that can and must be challenged politically and destabilized by the gay, lesbian, transgender and bisexual groups it stigmatized and excluded. The latter, in turn, must also destabilize their own stabilizations and exclusions of gender identities so as to further democratize and mobilize these. In this respect queer theory seems to differ from post-feminist and established gay or lesbian approaches in that it emphasizes the constant potential or actual 'bending' or 'queering' of sexual and gender orientations, rather than being an umbrella term for non-straight and post-feminist approaches.

This trajectory can be traced in film studies starting from Doane's notion of the masquerade, which informed the emergence of post-feminism. Contrary to Mulvey's contention that woman's visual presence is a dead-end for women spectators and her insistence that woman's only viable yet poor venue for voyeuristic pleasure and identification can be found in the male-protagonist-dominated narrative trajectory, Doane's masquerade, while still framed within Mulvey's claim that women figure in films mostly to be looked at, focused attention nevertheless upon the possible pleasures that woman's visual presence afforded women spectators. Moreover, as explained by Patricia White, 'for some theorists, if the woman's "visual presence tends to work against the development of a story line" … then it could be argued that spectacle itself could be understood as a weak link in the totalizing patriarchal regime Mulvey delineated and used as a way of interrupting narrative closure and its presumed confirmation of [male] spectatorial mastery'.[53] Hence, the growing post-feminist focus upon the spectacular aspect of film began to displace deconstructive feminist theories' insistence upon the domination of narrative trajectories and the attendant need to deconstruct these, a project perceived by post-feminists as leading to a dead-end.

Doane's post-feminist notion of the masquerade and the growing attention to film's spectacular portions coalesced with Butler's queer theory notion of performativity and performance and with the different strategies used by non-straight viewers to derive voyeuristic pleasure from films, strategies whose shared focus was upon the spectacular aspect of films. As pointed out by Patricia White, 'The musical genre's subordination of narrative codes to performance and spectacle might resist ideological containment, and this is possibly one source of its appeal to female and gay audiences.'[54] Hence, the film's narrative vectorial thrust was perceived as being constantly dismantled by the voyeuristic pleasures derived by differently gendered spectators from the polysemic and multidirectional nature of the film spectacle.

This focus upon spectacle engendered the growing attention to the spectacular film-star figure described by Richard Dyer as, 'unstable, never at a point of rest or equilibrium, constantly lurching from one formulation of what being human is to another'.[55] The multifaceted and polysemic phenomenon of film stars as complex configurations who operate beyond the confines of a film's narrative trajectory through their various intertextual references, and who apparently transgress the film-textual universe into the film stars' 'real' life, easily lends itself to a variety of voyeuristic pleasures for a variety of viewers' gender, sexual and ideological sensibilities.

This approach also opened the way to ethnographic and historical audience research of the simultaneous yet different decoding of the same film spectacle by real spectators of differing mixes of gender, ethnic and national attributes. This trend converged with the growing critique of film-text or film-as-apparatus oriented theories that postulated an abstract generalized viewer. In this respect, Stuart Hall's article 'Encoding/Decoding' offered the most powerful exposition of heterogeneous processes of textual decoding. In his analysis, the process whereby a message is produced or encoded in a text and the process whereby the text is decoded by the recipient are not univocal or complementary. In fact, 'it is possible for a viewer perfectly to understand both the literal and the connotative inflection given by a discourse but to decode the message in a *globally* contrary way. He/she detotalizes the message in the preferred code in order to retotalize the message within some alternative framework of reference.'[56]

In line with this approach, queer film theory began viewing film spectacles as the 'intersection or combination of more than one established "non-straight" sexuality or gender position in a spectator, a text, or a personality'.[57]

The focus upon film as spectacle and the attendant diversification of film spectators within post-feminist and queer theories revealed a variety of often contradicting voyeuristic pleasures. Hence, the pleasure derived by Doane's critical woman viewer's masquerading strategy may arguably apply to heterosexual women (since it presumes that women cannot enjoy their own image as object of desire and therefore need the critical distance afforded by masquerading), but it certainly does not apply to lesbian viewers much of whose voyeuristic pleasure derives precisely from viewing women as objects of desire. As noted by White, 'Lesbian spectatorship has posed a particularly revealing challenge to psychoanalytic theory's seeming equation of "sexual difference" with heterosexual complementarity – the presumption that women cannot desire the image because they *are* the image.'[58] Moreover, queer theory further detached voyeuristic pleasures from the long-held belief in a bond between the sexual or gender orientation of the viewer and that of the film protagonists in suggesting that 'viewers, no matter what their stated gender and sexuality identities, often position themselves "queerly" – that is, position themselves within gender and sexuality spaces other than those with which they publicly identify.'[59]

Queer theory found in film a major site of gender-performance propagation. The notion of gender as something unstable and fluid focused attention upon gender transgression or gender crises in films, while the notion of gender as performance drew attention to the film devices of irony, play and parody.[60]

2.3 FROM GENDER BENDING TO CYBORGS

Judith Butler's queer theory notion of gender and sexuality as floating signifiers not determined by the biological bodies they inhabit or by an essential-identity referent, logically coalesces with the computer-revolution-derived notion of the *cyborg*. As defined by Haraway, 'A cyborg is a cybernetic organism, a hybrid of machine and organism, a creature of social reality as well as a creature of fiction.'[61] Haraway found this mythical figure, with no clear origin or gender, embryonically materialized in each of us, given our species' evolving mutation through mechanical

Gender as Performance in *Some Like it Hot*

Some Like it Hot (1959), an emblematic film for queer theory, evidences the theory's attention to gender transgression or gender crises in films, as well as its notion of gender as performance through devices of irony, play and parody. The film tells the story of Joe and Jerry, two musicians on the run from the mob after witnessing the killing of several gangsters by their rivals in 1929 Chicago, leading them to dress as women and join an all-female jazz band performing in Miami. Once there, Joe (Tony Curtis), masquerading as Josephine, is attracted to Sugar (Marilyn Monroe), a musician in the band in search of a millionaire to marry. On the other hand, Jerry (Jack Lemon), masquerading as Daphne, is courted by Osgood Fielding III (Joe E. Brown), an aging playboy millionaire living on a yacht offshore. Joe poses as a millionaire and invites Sugar to 'his' yacht once he arranges for Jerry/Daphne to spend the night dancing with Osgood at a nightclub. While Daphna tangos with Osgood on the shore, we see in crosscutting Jerry seducing Sugar on Osgood's yacht by telling her he has lost all interest in women, leading Sugar to try to re-arouse his interest by kissing him deeply. Following a series of digressions and misunderstandings, Sugar finally learns of Jerry's true identity but they remain in love anyway. Daphne, on board Osgood's speedboat with them, reveals to Osgood that she is a he, to which Osgood, undisturbed and in love replies, 'Well, nobody's perfect.'

As can be seen, this comedy focuses upon deceptive identities, reversed sex roles and cross-dressing. In this it propagates a performative approach to gender. This comes through not only in the delight enjoyed by Joe

or animal implants. Born of the revolutionary conceptual impact brought about by computers and by the deciphering of the human genome, she detected its effects in the contemporary dismantling of the nuclear, biologically based model of the family. Now, when organs can be cloned and the cloning of humans is not very far off, the arbitrariness of gender attributions becomes more evident according to Haraway.

This does not mean, however, as implied by Michael Heim in his account of our fascination with computers, that cyborgs do not offer spectators voyeuristic pleasures:

> Our love affair with computers, computer graphics, and computer networks runs deeper than aesthetic fascination and deeper that the play of the senses. We are searching for a home for the mind and heart... The computer's allure is more than utilitarian or aesthetic; it is erotic ... our affair with information machines announces a symbiotic relationship and ultimately a mental marriage to technology.[62]

However, while Heim discussed technology in erotic terms and Haraway proposed to consider the post-human cyborg as a liberating, even socialist-feminist myth, its

and Jerry in their wearing female dresses, but is also enhanced through Jerry's shifts from 'female' dress to 'millionaire' dress, consisting of a yachting jacket and cap, the reading of the *Wall Street Journal*, and his speaking in an accent comically denoting sophistication. Moreover, while Sugar's highly sexualized figuration positions her as the ultimate erotic object of desire for both the viewers and the cross-dressed males (e.g. during the show, Sugar sings 'I Want to Be Loved By You' wearing a see-through dress as her breasts, partly shadowed by a spotlight move back and forth into the light), her appearance is also 'performatized' and somewhat desexualized due to the surrounding gender performances. This comes through particularly in the yacht scene, where Jerry's fake frigidity when Sugar kisses him again and again, conveys a dissonance

between her overflowing sexuality and Jerry's persuasive apathy. The film also deals comically with moments of gender transgression and crisis through the evolving relation between Jerry/Daphne and Osgood. This comes forth in particular during the scene following their tango night. Hence, once back in his room, Jerry, enchanted by his feminine performance and swept away by Osgood's marriage proposal (to which he agreed), is confronted by Joe who tells him it cannot be done since both Jerry and Osgood are males. At that point, Jerry, slowly coming to his 'senses', loses his equilibrium and as he sits down on the bed, the following dialogue ensues:

Joe: Just keep telling yourself you're a boy. You're a boy.
Jerry: I'm a boy.
Joe: That's the boy.

widespread film figuration in films like *Blade Runner*, *Strange Days* (1995), *Dark City* (1998) or the *Terminator* trilogy (1984, 1991, 2002) was usually couched in terms of the conservative opposition between humans and machines, offering technophobic and dystopic visions rather than liberating spectators from psychological constrains concerning gender or human-machine interaction.

2.4 A POST-MARXIST CRITIQUE OF QUEER AND CYBORG THEORIES

It seems that films lag behind the conceptual and aesthetic possibilities opened up by the emergent notion of the cyborg. On the other hand, from a post-Marxist point of view, it may well be that the human body, its materiality and *ensuing* desire, so tangibly communicated by films, is something we cannot, or should not give up. This tangible film presence and figuration subverts the abstractions that queer theory and the cyborg myth, through their respective notions of performance and machine, propagate. It may also subvert the far-fetched 'evenness' implied in their notion of 'performance' (e.g. a 'millionaire', a 'woman', a 'computer', or a 'poor man', for that matter), a notion that ultimately obscures the real unevenness in the current globalizing capitalist configurations of power.

Chapter Summary

Semiotic Psychoanalysis and Film

- The concept of *imaginary signifiers* brings together the semiotic aspect of film and its psychological effects.
- Metz noticed that film, mirror and dream are reflections of things perceived as tangible but lacking materiality.
- Metz applied Freud's four 'dream work' psychic procedures (*condensation, displacement, symbolization* and *secondary elaboration*) to film articulation.
- Complementing the neo-Marxist Althusserian notion of ideology with Lacanian psychoanalysis, Metz and others argued that films offer viewers an illusion of empowerment by leading them to rehearse the joyful infantile 'mirror stage' suggested by Lacan.
- Metz noted the viewers' identification with the point of view of a moving camera that creates a centred space converging into the viewer's eye.
- Dayan argued that the shot–counter-shot editing strategy 'sutures' the spectator's psyche to the film.

Deconstructive Feminism and Film

- Deconstructive feminists reacted against the 1960s' feminist biological essentialism by claiming that gender is structured by culture.
- Mulvey used Freud's psychoanalytic study of scopophilia to argue that male spectators identify with the male protagonist that leads the narrative and find erotic pleasure in watching the passive females that populate the spectacular portions of films, concluding that female spectators have no place in the theatre.
- Studlar suggested an altogether different explanation for female viewing pleasure based on masochism.
- Doane found the perception of female protagonists as masquerading 'femininity' to be an effective way of opening a distance from the female image, turning it manipulable by women spectators.

Post-feminist and Queer Theory

- Post-feminists offered an understanding of femininity as a fluid rather than fixed identity. This coalesced with queer theories that addressed gay, lesbian, bisexual and transgender sensibilities, while criticizing the long-held binary opposition of male to female identities.
- Judith Butler defined gender as *performance* rather than as an inextricably fixed identity.
- Post-feminism and queer theories focused upon the multifaceted characteristic of the film spectacle and its 'opening' to different gender and sexual sensibilities on account of the previous focus upon film's linear narrative trajectory and the presumption of a generalized abstract viewer.
- The research of the film spectacle engendered the study of spectacular film stars who 'open' the film to coincidental readings by viewers with different gender and sexual orientations, leading also to specific ethnographic and historical research of different constituents of the viewing audiences.
- The queer theory notion of gender coalesces with the computer-revolution-derived notion of the *cyborg* as defined by Haraway, a mythical half-human/half-machine figure with no clear origin or gender.

QUESTIONS FOR ESSAYS AND CLASS DISCUSSION

1 FROM THE PHOTOGENIC TO THE SIMULACRUM

1. Can films reveal hidden aspects of the reality they record? Discuss the different answers provided to this question by Epstein, Vertov and Baudrillard.
2. What is the relation of the photogenic to film art? Discuss how Bazin's conception of this relation differs from that of Tynjanov.
3. On what grounds did Marxists critique Bazin's realism and Tynjanov's formalism?
4. How does the digital revolution in film, evident in films like Andy and Larry Wachowski's *The Matrix* (1999), affect the cinematic conception of reality?
5. Discuss the documentary and fictional aspects of Michael Moore's film *Fahrenheit 9/11* (2004).

2 FILM CONSTRUCTS

1. What is the nature of film signs? Discuss the different answers provided to this question by Barthes, Metz and Wollen.
2. Do films have 'deep structures'? Discuss the structural and poststructural positions on this question, particularly as they relate to the notion of film genres.
3. How is meaning construed in the interaction between film and spectator? Compare Ben-Porath's intertextual method to Bordwell's cognitive approach.
4. Using Noel Carroll's 'question-and-answer' model, can you explain how Christopher Nolan's film *Memento* (2000) cues the spectator to construct in his/her mind its temporal construction?

5. Discern and discuss the fairy-tale intertextual relations in Andrew Adamson's and Vicky Jenson's film *Shrek* (2001).

3 DIALECTIC FILM MONTAGE

1. Do films manipulate spectators ideologically? Compare the formalist and cognitivist positions on this question to the Marxist one.
2. Why is dialectic film montage an effective ideological manipulation according to Eisenstein?
3. What is the nature of 'aura' in film according to Benjamin? Discuss the aura of film stars such as Bruce Willis or Julia Roberts.
4. How do continuity edited films manipulate spectators according to Baudry or Heath?
5. In Jameson's terms, is David Fincher's film *Fight Club* (1999) a postmodern film? Is it a progressive or regressive film according to Jameson?

4 IMAGINARY SIGNIFIERS/VOYEURISTIC PLEASURES

1. On what basis are films compared to dreams or mirrors? Discuss the presumed dreamlike or mirror-like influences of films on spectators.
2. Why did Mulvey claim that 'classical narrative films' discriminate against women?
3. Is female 'masquerading' in films a subversive strategy?
4. Is gender natural or 'performed'? In what sense do films support Butler's notion of 'gender as performance'?
5. In queer theory terms, what spectatorial positions can be assumed when watching Ang Lee's film *Brokeback Mountain* (2005)?

NOTES

I FROM THE PHOTOGENIC TO THE SIMULACRUM

1. Rudolph Arnheim, *Art and Visual Perception* (Berkeley: University of California Press, 1967), pp. 52–3.
2. See a similar position in Noel Burch, *Theory of Film Practice* (Princeton, NJ: Princeton University Press, 1981).
3. Stuart E. Liebman, *Jean Epstein's Early Film Theory, 1920–1922* (New York University Dissertation, Ann Arbor, MI: University Microfilms International, 1983), p. 132.
4. Liebman, *Jean Epstein's Early Film Theory*, p. 117.
5. Liebman, *Jean Epstein's Early Film Theory*, p. 227.
6. Liebman, *Jean Epstein's Early Film Theory*, p. 231.
7. Roland Barthes, 'The Photographic Message', in *Image, Music, Text* (New York: Hill and Wang, 1978), pp. 30–1. Barthes's semiology is discussed in Chapter 2.
8. Balazs offers an emblematic example of the realists' presupposition of mystery in his description of the facial close-up where 'we can see there is something there that we can't see'. See Bela Balazs, *Theory of the Film: Character and Growth of a New Art* (New York: Dover Publications, 1970), p. 76.
9. A detailed analysis of Vertov's theory appears in Chapter 3.
10. Liebman addresses the relation between Epstein's photogenie and Benjamin's aura (Liebman, *Jean Epstein's Early Film Theory*, pp. 231–2). On Benjamin's reflections on film, see Chapter 3.
11. Walter Benjamin, 'The Work of Art in the Age of Mechanical Reproduction', in H. Arendt (ed.), *Illuminations* (New York: Shocken Books, 1969), p. 236.
12. André Bazin, 'The Ontology of the Photographic Image', in *What is Cinema? Volume I* (Berkeley: University of California Press, 1967), pp. 9–16.
13. André Bazin, 'The Evolution of the Language of Cinema', in *What is Cinema?* pp. 23–40.
14. Bazin, 'Ontology of the Photographic Image', p. 12.
15. Bazin, 'Ontology of the Photographic Image', p. 12.
16. Bazin, 'Ontology of the Photographic Image', p. 13.
17. Bazin, 'Ontology of the Photographic Image', p. 15.
18. Bazin, 'Ontology of the Photographic Image', p. 16.
19. Bazin, 'Evolution of the Language of Cinema', p. 24.
20. Bazin, 'Evolution of the Language of Cinema', p. 34.
21. Bazin, 'Evolution of the Language of Cinema', p. 36.
22. Bazin, 'Ontology of the Photographic Image', p. 14.
23. James Roy MacBean, 'Vent d'est or Godard and Rocha at the Crossroads', in B. Nichols (ed.), *Movies and Methods* (Berkeley: University of California Press, 1985), pp. 95–6.

24. On Althusser and neo-Marxist film theory, see Chapter 3.

25. On Noel Carroll and cognitivist film theory, see Chapter 2.

26. See Lee T. Lemon and Marion J. Reis, *Russian Formalist Criticism: Four Essays* (London: University of Nebraska Press, 1965), p. 12. Victor Shklovsky along with Boris Eichenbaum were two of the leading figures who founded the first formalist group *Opoyaz* (which stands in Russian for 'The Society for the Study of Poetic Language') in St Petersburg in 1914, followed by the Moscow Linguistic Circle, which included Roman Jacobson and Boris Tomashevsky. Their main focus was literature.

27. Y. Tynjanov, 'The Foundations of Cinema', in H. Eagle (ed.), *Russian Formalist Film Theory* (Ann Arbor: Michigan Slavic Publications, 1981), pp. 97–8.

28. Boris Kazanskij, 'The Nature of Cinema', in H. Eagle (ed.), *Russian Formalist Film Theory* (Ann Arbor: Michigan Slavic Publications, 1981), p. 103.

29. Hence, Eichenbaum dealt with film style; Tynjanov with the foundations of cinema; Kazanskij compares film to other arts; Piotrovskij writes on film genres and Shklovsky on poetry and prose in cinema.

30. Tynjanov, 'Foundations of Cinema', pp. 81–100.

31. Tynjanov, 'Foundations of Cinema', p. 81.

32. Tynjanov, 'Foundations of Cinema', p. 90.

33. Tynjanov, 'Foundations of Cinema', p. 86.

34. Tynjanov, 'Foundations of Cinema', p. 85.

35. Tynjanov, 'Foundations of Cinema', p. 85.

36. Tynjanov, 'Foundations of Cinema', p. 87.

37. Tynjanov, 'Foundations of Cinema', p. 87.

38. Tynjanov, 'Foundations of Cinema', p. 100.

39. There have been powerful cinematic historical dramas, such as Oliver Hirschbiegel's recent film *The Downfall: Hitler and the End of the Third Reich* (2004) where Bruno Ganz establishes a resemblance to Hitler while powerfully conveying Hitler's murderous politics. This may be due, in Tynjanov's terms, to a loosened attribution of truth to referential film images in the age of digitization.

40. Tynjanov, 'Foundations of Cinema', p. 100. Tynjanov's Russian formalist consideration of film genres was further explored by Piotrovskij who offered a typology of genres in his time based upon the degree of their stemming from specific film devices. Hence, he valued silent comedies due to their being based upon fragmentation and upon play with props as actors, and rejected psychological dramas due to their being based upon non-visual complex psychological motivations.

41. While Eisenstein was referring to Vertov's film *Man with a Movie Camera*, which he didn't really understand (see A. Michelson (ed.), *Kino-Eye, the Writings of Dziga Vertov* , Berkeley: University of California Press, 1984, pp. xx–xxiii), his type of critique seems more appropriate to Walther Ruttman's film *Berlin, symphony of a city* (1927), a film which like Vertov's focused on the rhythms of the modern city, but unlike it, dealt with rhythmical abstractions irrespective of sociopolitical considerations.

42. Burch, *Theory of Film Practice*, p. vi.

43. We will consider the positions of the Marxist-oriented thinkers of the Frankfurt School on formalism in Chapter 2.

44. Benjamin, 'Work of Art in the Age of Mechanical Reproduction', p. 242.

45. Jean Baudrillard, *For a Critique of the Political Economy of the Sign* (St. Louis, MO: Telos, 1981), p. 155.

46. Hayden White, *Tropics of Discourse: Essays in Cultural Criticism* (Baltimore: John Hopkins University Press, 1978).

47. See Thomas S. Kuhn, *The Structure of Scientific Revolutions* (Chicago: University of Chicago Press, 1970).

48. Jean Baudrillard, 'Simulacra and Simulations', in M. Poster (ed.), *Selected Writings* (Stanford: Stanford University Press, 1988), pp. 166–84.

49. Baudrillard, 'Simulacra and Simulations', pp. 180–1.

50. Vivian Sobchack, 'At the Still Point of the Turning World' in V. Sobchack (ed.), *Meta-Morphing* (Minnesota: Minnesota University Press, 2000), p. 142.

2 FILM CONSTRUCTS

1. Two basic formalist principles were highly influential in the development of structural semiology and structuralism: the principle concerning the shift from the ordinary, natural context to the artistic one was incorporated into these theories' attempts at typologizing the medium's ways of conveying meaning in their assumption that the value of film components derived less from their extra-cinematic origin and more from their mutual structural interrelation in groups of films, or from their interrelation in cinema's specific sign system. This latter semiological premise was derived from the formalists' idea that each art form has its own specific means of production, a premise leading semiologists such as Christian Metz to base their search after cinema's specific sign system on the sole basis of their particular, unique material signifiers such as recorded images coupled with recorded sounds imparting motion, and specific editing signifiers such as cuts and dissolves.

2. Ferdinand de Saussure, *Course in General Linguistics* (New York: McGraw-Hill, 1966).

3. Jonathan Culler, *Structuralist Poetics* (Ithaca, NY: Cornell University Press, 1975), p. 6, writes in this excellent survey of structuralism, that 'It would not be wrong to suggest that structuralism and semiology are identical.'

4. For a survey of Saussure's principles and their semiological development see R. Barthes, *Elements of Semiology* (New York: Hill and Wang, 1964).

5. Claude Lévi-Strauss, 'Structure and Form: Reflections on a Work by Vladimir Propp', in *Structural Anthropology, Volume 2* (Chicago: The University of Chicago Press, 1983), p. 115. While Lévi-Strauss here addresses Propp's *Formalism*, his comments are applicable to what he would have considered to be a similarly unwarranted differentiation *within* the sign between the privileged signifier (i.e. form) and its arbitrarily related signified (i.e. content). For Lévi-Strauss signs are inseparable form-content units. While letters are forms without content, words are not, and while the relation between signifier and signified in a word may be 'arbitrary', it is constant and inseparable within the structure of language.

6. Saussure, *Course in General Linguistics*, p. 68.

7. Barthes, *Elements of Semiology*, pp. 40–51.

8. Roland Barthes, 'Myth Today', in *Mythologies* (Paris: Editions du Seuil, 1972). Neo-Marxists based their critique of film upon the premise that film naturalizes ideology. See Chapter 3.

9. See Christian Metz's *Film Language* (Oxford: Oxford University Press, 1974) and his 'On the Notion of Cinematographic Language', in Bill Nichols (ed.), *Movies and Methods* (Berkeley: University of California Press, 1976).

10. Umberto Eco suggested that film images consist of a triple articulation: the first level of articulation consists in his view of discrete graphic signs such as circular or straight lines. These are combined

into more complex discrete iconic signs such as an eye, formed by circular combinations. The combination of these iconic signs generates, on a third level of articulation, meaningful units (semes) such as when you put one eye to the side of another, a nose beneath and in-between the eyes, and a mouth right below the nose. The complexity involved in triple articulations was taken by Eco to explain the apparent analogical fullness perceived in photographs. He went on to suggest that films connect these synchronic images diachronically to create complex articulations through motion. Umberto Eco, 'Articulations of the Cinematic Code', in Nichols, *Movies and Methods*, pp. 590–607.

11. Metz, *Film Language, p.* 146.
12. Metz, 'Cinematographic Language', pp. 587–8.
13. Metz himself offers an example of a durative syntagm describing the tenuous crossing of a dessert in a western film ('Cinematographic Language', pp. 587–8).
14. Peter Wollen, 'The Semiology of the Cinema', in *Signs and Meaning in the Cinema* (Bloomington, Indiana: Indiana University Press, 1972), pp. 116–54.
15. Wollen, 'Semiology of the Cinema', pp. 141–3. Wollen, following Roman Jacobson, detailed a variety of instances in language where utterances mimic natural order. Not only onomatopoeias evidence such mimicry, but traces can also be found in the fact that most languages use more letters in the plural, and in their including stable linguistic idioms like 'veni, vidi, vici' that follow the sequence of events in the world. Moreover, argued Wollen, it is almost impossible to understand linguistic utterances without knowing who speaks, when and where, a knowledge that cannot be solely derived from Saussure's insulated language system.
16. The American philosopher Charles Sanders Peirce developed his semiotic theory at around the same time that Saussure developed his structural linguistics.
17. J. Buchler (ed.), *Philosophical Writings of Peirce* (New York: Dover Publications, Inc., 1955), p. 106. Peirce offered ten trichotomies of the sign but his second trichotomy is considered his most important contribution and is the one that most influenced film studies.
18. Wollen, 'Semiology of the Cinema', p. 123.
19. Wollen, 'Semiology of the Cinema', p. 143.
20. Wollen, 'Semiology of the Cinema', p. 137.
21. Wollen, 'Semiology of the Cinema', p. 154.
22. Wollen, 'Semiology of the Cinema', p. 141.
23. Culler in *Structuralist Poetics* offers a critical evaluation of major structuralists including Saussure, Claude Lévi-Strauss and Tzvetan Todorov. Jean Piaget, however, is mentioned by Culler in one single footnote.
24. Claude Lévi-Strauss, 'The Structural Study of Myth', in *Structural Anthropology* (New York: Basic Books Inc., 1963), pp. 206–31.
25. This bounding principle was the major site of attack by poststructuralists. As will be seen in Chapter 2, section 2, it is very difficult to legitimize the delineation of boundaries to a cultural system. Lévi-Strauss himself conceded this to be a problem.
26. The binary principle was considered by Lévi-Strauss as well as by Saussure and other structuralists as a central logical and practical faculty of language. Lévi-Strauss considered it to be the major way humans think. The Russian formalist Tynjanov (see Chapter 1) also insinuated binary oppositions when claiming that choosing the things to be seen in film derives from stylistic-semantic considerations based on the 'contrastive and differential' mutual characteristics of the objects or actors chosen rather than from their social or other extra-filmic consideration. Nevertheless, neither Tynjanov nor other formalists developed this premise systematically.

27. Lévi-Strauss, 'Reflections on a Work by Vladimir Propp', p. 115.

28. He likened this to the reconstruction of the synchronic pack of cards used by fortune-tellers through the statistical recurrence of their diachronic predictions (Lévi-Strauss, 'Structural Study of Myth', p. 212).

29. Lévi-Strauss confessed to not being an expert in Greek mythology and likened his work to that of a street peddler 'whose aim is not to achieve a concrete result, but to explain, as succinctly as possible, the functioning of the mechanical toy which he is trying to sell to the on-lookers' ('Structural Study of Myth', p. 213).

30. While Lévi-Strauss likens his gross constituent units to 'lower' language levels comprised of signifiers without signifieds (e.g. phonemes), he bypasses Saussure's 'vertical' signifier/signified split within the sign and maintains only the similarity on the 'horizontal' relational structure. This is his main divergence from semiologists like Metz who gave up on studying such 'gross' units on the level of the film's image contents since he couldn't find this 'vertical' split in their continuous and analogous articulation.

31. Lévi-Strauss, 'Structural Study of Myth', p. 216.

32. In studying the versions of the North American Zuñi tribe myth dealing with the irresolvable contradiction between life and death, Lévi-Strauss discerned another mythical operation whereby units representing death (e.g. carnivorous animals) figure within the same column 'above' units representing life (vegetarian animals), but then converge into a column consisting of one unit that includes both (an animal both carnivorous and vegetarian). This unit, which he called 'the trickster', inverts the poles of life and death so that in the next column the positions of life units appear 'above' those representing death. Thus, the myth, by inverting the columns ends up saying that life and death are not opposed to each other since we find that life representing units mutate to death ones and that life inhabits death. As will be seen, the western genre protagonist is such a 'trickster' unit in-between civilization and nature.

33. Thomas Schatz, 'The structural Influence: New Directions in Film Genre Study', in B. K. Grant (ed.), Film Genre Reader II (Austin: University of Texas Press, 1995), p. 99. See also in Schatz an overview of structural approaches to film.

34. The first to have noticed this conflict was probably Henry Nash Smith in his book Virgin Land (Cambridge MA: Harvard University Press, 1950), where he unearths this contradiction in the writings of James Fennimore Cooper.

35. See above, note 32.

36. Wollen, 'The Auteur Theory', in Signs and Meaning in the Cinema (Bloomington, IN: Indiana University Press, 1972), p. 80.

37. Wollen, 'Auteur Theory', pp. 72–115.

38. Wollen, 'Auteur Theory', p. 81.

39. Wollen, 'Auteur Theory', p. 81.

40. Wollen, 'Auteur Theory', p. 96.

41. Wollen, 'Auteur Theory', p. 96.

42. Vladimir Propp, Morphology of the Folktale, ed. L. Wagner (Austin: University of Texas Press, 1968).

43. Propp, Morphology of the Folktale, pp. 20–1.

44. Propp, Morphology of the Folktale, pp. 114, 128.

45. Propp, Morphology of the Folktale, p. 54.

46. Will Wright, Sixguns and Society (Berkeley: University of California Press, 1975).

47. The term poststructuralism subsumes a wide range of positions some of them even contradicting. The following discussion focuses upon premises more or less shared by different leading poststructuralists.

48. See Michel Foucault's 'Truth and Power', in P. Rabinow (ed.), *The Foucault Reader* (New York: Pantheon Books, 1984), pp. 101–2.

49. Steve Neal, 'Questions of Genre', in B. K. Grant (ed.), *Film Genre Reader II* (Austin: University of Texas Press, 1995), pp. 159–83.

50. Rick Altman, 'A Semantic/Syntactic Approach to Film Genre', in Grant, *Film Genre Reader II*, p. 34.

51. Altman, 'Semantic/Syntactic Approach', pp. 26–41.

52. See Julia Kristeva, 'The Bounded Text', in *Desire in Language* (New York: Columbia University Press, 1980), p. 111.

53. Kristeva, 'The Bounded Text', p. 36.

54. See Roland Barthes, *Image, Music, Text* (Glasgow: Fontana, 1977), p 157.

55. See Gerard Genette, *Palimpsestes, La Litterature au Second Degre* (Paris: Editions du Seuil, 1982).

56. Ziva Ben-Porath, 'Intertextuality' in *Hassifrut*, 1983 (34), 2 [Hebrew].

57. Noel Carroll critiques this widespread poststructural attitude towards truth and objectivity.

58. See Noel Carroll, *Mystifying Movies, Fads and Fallacies in Contemporary Film Theory* (New York: Columbia University Press, 1988), pp. 188–99.

59. For example, Carroll, *Mystifying Movies*. His critique is reviewed in Chapters 3 and 4.

60. Carroll, *Mystifying Movies*, pp. 138–47, 170–81, 199–212.

61. David Bordwell, *Narration in the Fiction Film* (Madison, WI: University of Wisconsin Press, 1985), pp. 29–47.

62. Bordwell, as well as other cognitivists, was influenced in this definition of film's enjoyment by the formalist premise that the function of art is to challenge and play with the perceiver's cognitive activities. From early precursors of cognitive film theory such as Rudolph Arnheim to David Bordwell the search for the viewer's cognitive processes while watching a film was premised upon film's posing of cognitive challenges to the viewers, leading them to construct the film in their minds. Moreover, for cognitivists as for the formalists, the viewer's aesthetic enjoyment of film derived from these perceptual and cognitive challenges.

63. Edward Brannigan, *Narrative Comprehension and Film* (London: Routledge, 1992) offers the most elaborated cognitivist theory of narrative.

64. Bordwell borrowed the term from the Russian formalists. He also borrowed from them the differentiation between story and plot formations as well as the relation between style, plot and genre (see Chapter 1). Unlike the formalists, however, Bordwell did not use these concepts to explain an insulated film, but to explain the dynamic interaction whereby different film genres help the viewers to construct a film's narrative in their mind.

65. For Carroll's counter-critique of neo-Marxism, see Chapter 3.

66. Film cognitivists conceded that their approach initially disregarded emotions. However, Carroll as well as others have since then tried to implement in film studies cognitive theories of emotion.

3 DIALECTIC FILM MONTAGE

1. For example, Noel Burch, *Theory of Film Practice* (Princeton, NJ: Princeton University Press, 1981). While Burch explicitly founded his neo-formalist film aesthetic upon dialectic configurations,

dialectic film montage corresponds in some of its aspects to the formalist notion of estrangement or unfamiliarity in art.

2. Wollen, for example, mentions John Ford's image in *The Man Who Shot Liberty Valance* (1962) of a cactus rose 'which encapsulates the antinomy between desert and garden'. See 'The Auteur Theory', in *Signs and Meaning in the Cinema* (Bloomington, IN: Indiana University Press, 1972), p. 96.

3. I describe them as formal because they consider the dialectic as a peculiar property of works of art or cultural systems, excluding extra-cultural or artistic factors.

4. As will be noticed, the trajectory traced from a Marxist constructivist dialectic film montage to a decentred postmodernism, overlaps the shift from structural to poststructural theory delineated in Chapter 2.

5. Karl Marx and Friedrich Engels, *The German Ideology* (New York: International Publishers, 1947), p. 42.

6. Marx & Engels, *The German Ideology*, p. 73.

7. See Karl Marx, 'Economic and Philosophical Manuscripts', in *Early Writings* (Harmondsworth: Penguin Books, 1975), p. 351.

8. Sergei M. Eisenstein, 'A Dialectic Approach to Film Form', in *Film Form* (New York: HBJ Books, 1949), pp. 45–64.

9. From a Marxist point of view, art has always a social function. Formalism in the arts, in its attempts to exclude sociopolitical concerns from the study of art was not only turning away from art's (necessary) social function but was also encouraging a-social behaviour, conforming to the abstract mentality of the exploiting classes. The Marxist critiques of formalism are discussed throughout this chapter.

10. Eisenstein, 'Dialectic Approach', p. 48.

11. Eisenstein, 'Dialectic Approach', pp. 57–8.

12. Goebbels is quoted by Siegfried Kracauer in his book *From Caligari to Hitler, a Psychological History of the German Film* (Princeton, NJ: Princeton University Press, 1947, pp. 289–90) in the context of a comparison between Eisenstein's film and Leni Riefenstahl's Nazi propaganda film *Triumph of the Will* (1935).

13. Eisenstein described his filmmaking in opposition to Vertov's *kinoglaz (film-eye)* as a *film-fist*. His focus was upon dialectic process he presumed to be effectively rehearsed in the interaction between spectator and a cinematic montage of conflicts. Vertov on the other hand focused less on this interaction and more in the cinematic 'research' of reality.

14. See Annette Michelson (ed.), *Kino-Eye, the Writings of Dziga Vertov* (Berkeley: University of California Press, 1984), p. xxx. This exposition of Vertov's positions is partly indebted to Annette Michelson's introduction to her book on Vertov.

15. Marx & Engels, *The German Ideology*, p. 58.

16. Michelson, *Kino-Eye*, pp. 47, 66.

17. The notion of film as a 'Truth Machine' is widespread during the 1920s. See the discussion of the photogenic in Chapter 1.

18. Michelson, *Kino-Eye*, p. 41.

19. Michelson, *Kino-Eye*, p. 91.

20. This conception of rhythm was shared by many at the time, particularly by Soviet constructivists as can be found in Mayakovski's poetry or in Vladimir Tatlin's model of the 'Monument for the Third International', which was intended as a huge spirally revolving construction described by Shklovsky as made of 'iron, glass and revolution'. See Michelson, *Kino-Eye*, p. xxxiii.

21. Walter Benjamin, 'The Work of Art in the Age of Mechanical Reproduction', in H. Arendt (ed.), *Illuminations* (New York: Shocken Books, 1969), pp. 217–52.

22. Benjamin, 'Work of Art in the Age of Mechanical Reproduction', p. 218.

23. Benjamin's position that the artistic avant-garde ends up serving fascism was rejected by several Frankfurt School members such as Adorno, Horkheimer and Marcuse. Adorno rejected his detection of revolutionary trends in popular culture (e.g. in Chaplin's films). For Adorno and Horkheimer, popular culture in the capitalist world was a *culture industry* pumping capitalist ideology into the exploited masses' minds. See Theodor Adorno and Max Horkheimer, 'The Culture Industry: Enlightenment as Mass Deception', in *Dialectics of Enlightenment* (London: Verso, 1986), pp. 120–67. Also, contrary to the traditional Marxist position on formalism adhered to by Benjamin, they did find in the artistic avant-garde's constant search for new forms of expression an attempt to defrost aesthetic and mental fixations, thereby inadvertently promoting a revolutionary mentality.

24. Antonio Gramsci, *Selections from the Prison Notebooks* (London: Lawrence & Wishart).

25. Louis Althusser, 'Ideology and Ideological State Apparatuses', in *Lenin and Philosophy* (New York: MRP, 1971), p. 159.

26. Althusser, 'Ideology and Ideological State Apparatuses', pp. 127–88.

27. Jacques Lacan, 'The Mirror Stage as Formative of the Function of the I', in *Ecrits, a Selection* (New York: W.W. Norton and Company, 1977). For more on Lacan, see Chapter 4.

28. Cognitivists harshly critiqued what Noel Carroll has termed the Althusserian–Lacanian paradigm in film studies. Carroll dismisses Althusser's notion of ideology as too encompassing and conflated with the wider concept of culture. This conception doesn't leave any way out of the ideological immersion people are presumed to be in nor does it allow for any meaningful rejection of an ideology. He therefore suggests a return to the simple definition according to which ideology is a conscious manipulation. This allows for a clearer demarcation between ideology in a film and non-ideological aspects in film. Moreover, asks Carroll, in what sense has Althusser gone beyond classical Marxism if the latter actually provides a simple answer to why the exploited do not revolt? Doesn't it make more sense, he suggests, to presume that the exploited do not revolt because they are afraid to lose their jobs or lives? Why is there a need to develop complex theories of ideological manipulation? See Noel Carroll, *Mystifying Movies, Fads and Fallacies in Contemporary Film Theory* (New York: Columbia University Press), pp. 53–88.

29. Jean Louis Baudry, 'Ideological Effects of the Basic Cinematographic Apparatus', in Bill Nichols (ed.), *Movies and Methods Volume II* (Berkeley: University of California Press, 1985), pp. 531–42.

30. For a non-ideological reading of linear (and synthetic) perspective in relation to film, see David Bordwell, *Narration in the Fiction Film* (Madison, WI: University of Wisconsin Press, 1985), pp. 5–7. Cognitivists like Carroll rejected the notion that spectators identify with the camera leading them to feel that they originate the movie. If such was the case, asks Carroll, how can it be that the spectator is in a state of suspense concerning future developments? Why should they guess about something they originate? Likewise Carroll rejects the neo-Marxist notion that the homogenized, centred space 'positions' a centred subject that cannot help but yield to ideological manipulations. Even presuming that the space is centred and that the spectator perceives it as such, says Carroll, it does not follow that he must accept the image of reality represented. Spectators can perceive a centred space and reject the reality represented. The spectator, contends Carroll, is not a simple effect of the film. Carroll rejects the whole notion that linear perspective creates a *fraudulent* illusion. While it does offer an illusion of three-dimensionality, this illusion is not an ideological *convention* that colonized culture (a notion implying there could be as easily other forms of representation). Linear perspective, says Carroll, is a rather useful cultural *invention* fitted to human sight. It allows us to learn about the *real* world around us. See Carroll, *Mystifying Movies*, pp. 53–88.

31. Stephen Heath, 'Narrative Space' in *Questions of Cinema* (Bloomington, IN: Indiana University Press, 1981), pp. 19–75.
32. Further examples of Godard's deconstructive strategies can be found in James Roy MacBean, 'Vent d'est or Godard and Rocha at the Crossroads', in Bill Nichols (ed.), *Movies and Methods* (Berkeley: University of California Press, 1985), pp. 91–110.
33. Frantz Fanon, *The Wretched of the Earth* (New York: Grove Press, 1967).
34. Fanon, *The Wretched of the Earth*, p. 40.
35. Fanon, *The Wretched of the Earth*, p. 46.
36. For example, Fernando Solanas's and Octavio Getino's Argentine film *Hour of the Furnaces* (1968); Thomas Gutierrez Alea's Cuban film *Memories of underdevelopment* (1968), Yucef Shahin's Egyptian film *The Sparrow* (1973) or Ousmane Sembene's Senegalese film *Xala* (1975).
37. See a reading of this scene and of the film as a whole from an anti-colonial perspective in Robert Stam and Louis Spence, 'Colonialism, Racism, and Representation: An Introduction', in Bill Nichols (ed.), *Movies and Methods Vol. 2* (Berkeley: University of California Press, 1985).
38. Fredric Jameson, *Post-Modernism, Or, the Cultural Logic of Late Capitalism* (Durham, NC: Duke University Press, 1991); David Harvey, *The Condition of Postmodernity* (Cambridge, MA: Blackwell, 2001).
39. A good example is *Austin Powers, the Spy Who Shagged Me* (1999), which offers a nostalgic return to an idealized, explicitly fake image of the 1960s' period through intertextual references to James Bond films.
40. Homi K. Bhaba, *The Location of Culture* (London: Routledge, 1994).

4 IMAGINARY SIGNIFIERS/VOYEURISTIC PLEASURES

1. Rudolph Arnheim, *Film as Art* (Berkeley: University of California Press, 1957), p. 3.
2. David Bordwell, *Narration in the Fiction Film* (Madison: University of Wisconsin Press, 1985); Noel Carroll, *Mystifying Movies, Fads and Fallacies in Contemporary Film Theory* (New York: Columbia University Press, 1988).
3. Stuart E. Liebman, *Jean Epstein's Early Film Theory, 1920–1922* (New York University Dissertation, Ann Arbor, MI: University Microfilms International, 1983), p. 55.
4. The likening of films to dreams has accompanied the medium since its inception. See Charles F. Altman, 'Psychoanalysis and Cinema: The Imaginary Discourse', in Bill Nichols (ed.), *Movies and Methods Vol. 2* (Berkeley: University of California Press, 1985), pp. 524–6.
5. Freud described how dreams appear to us using the metaphor of film projection, as quoted in Jean Louis Baudry, 'Ideological Effects of the Basic Cinematographic Apparatus', in Bill Nichols (ed.), *Movies and Methods Volume II* (Berkeley: University of California Press, 1985), p. 532.
6. Sigmund Freud, *Interpretation of Dreams* (New York: Avon Books, 1965).
7. Jacques Lacan, 'The Mirror Stage as Formative of the Function of the I', in *Ecrits, a Selection* (New York: W.W. Norton and Company, 1977), pp. 1–8.
8. Freud, *Interpretation of Dreams*, p. 177.
9. Freud, *Interpretation of Dreams*, pp. 311–546.
10. Freud, *Interpretation of Dreams*, p. 330.
11. Freud, *Interpretation of Dreams*, p. 389.
12. Freud, *Interpretation of Dreams*, p. 258.
13. Freud, *Interpretation of Dreams*, p. 587.

14. Freud, *Interpretation of Dreams*, p. 607.
15. The term cathexis was used by Freud to describe the process whereby a dreamer concentrates in an idea or thought charged with psychical energy (*Interpretation of Dreams*, p. 210, fn. 1).
16. Freud himself offers this correlation when comparing dream censorship to the social censorship of art (*Interpretation of Dreams*, pp. 175–7).
17. The psychoanalyst Jacques Lacan hypothesized that the unconscious is built like a language. Hence he maintained that the linguistic devices of metaphor and metonymy are to be compared or understood as Freud understood condensations and displacements in dreams (compared by Metz respectively to film dissolves and cuts). See Christian Metz, *The Imaginary Signifier* (Bloomington, IN: Indiana University Press, 1982), pp. 281–92.
18. Surrealists, claiming there is no ontological difference between dream and reality, relied heavily upon Freud's psychoanalytic theory of dreams. They also valued the medium of film because it allowed them to place real-looking objects in configurations that were impossible in reality, as they also practised in painting such as René Magritte's painting of a train rushing out of a cemented fireplace or Salvador Dali's drawings of melting clocks.
19. This same premise underlines neo-Marxist critiques of narrative continuous films as sweeping spectators away through their apparent continuity and henceforth effectively inculcating in them their ideology (see Chapter 3).
20. Lacan, 'Mirror Stage', p. 2.
21. Lacan, 'Mirror Stage', p. 2.
22. This is one of the sources of human desire. The notion of frustrated desires is cardinal to Lacan's psychoanalysis.
23. Lacan had reservations concerning the Freudian understanding of the Ideal Ego (see Lacan, 'Mirror Stage', p. 7 fn. 1). Hence, whereas Lacan attributes the initial formation of the Ideal Ego already to the mirror stage, Freud attributed it to the Oedipal stage during which humans acquire a sense of gender and the boy in particular internalizes the figure of the father as Ideal Ego or *superego* (see on the Oedipus complex in the section dealing with Laura Mulvey).
24. Lacan, 'Mirror Stage', p. 2.
25. Jacques Lacan, *Ecrits, a Selection* (New York: W.W. Norton and Company, 1977), pp. 103–4.
26. On Lacan's modes of cognition and their relation to Freudian stages of maturation see Lacan, *Ecrits*, pp. ix–xi; Metz, *Imaginary Signifier*, pp. 81–2, fn. 9.
27. See Chapter 3. See also Baudry, 'Ideological Effects'; Heath, 'Narrative Space'.
28. Christian Metz, 'Story/Discourse: Notes on Two Kinds of Voyeurism', in Bill Nichols (ed.), *Movies and Methods Vol. 2* (Berkeley: University of California Press, 1985), pp. 543–9.
29. Metz, 'Story/Discourse', pp. 548–9. The concepts mentioned belong to Freud's mapping of the human psyche into the ego, the superego and the id. It overlaps Freud's other mapping of the psyche into the conscious and the unconscious. The *id* is the unconscious, the source of instinctual energies.
30. Daniel Dayan, 'The Tutor Code of Classical Cinema', in Bill Nichols (ed.), *Movies and Methods* (Berkeley: University of California Press, 1976), pp. 438–51.
31. The notion that editing transitions threaten the film's illusion and the attendant disruption of film's manipulation of viewers has also generated different variations. See the discussion of Baudry's and Heath's positions in Chapter 3, where it is also shown how Lacanian-derived psychoanalytic theories of film informed Althusserian neo-Marxist film research.
32. In Greek mythology the nymph Echo had the power to generate speech, but was punished by jealous Juno who relegated her to the reproduction of sounds made by others.

33. Altman, 'Psychoanalysis and Cinema', pp. 528–9.
34. Altman, 'Psychoanalysis and Cinema', pp. 530–1.
35. Carroll, *Mystifying Movies*.
36. Laura Mulvey, 'Visual Pleasure and Narrative Cinema', in Bill Nichols (ed.), *Movies and Methods Vol. 2* (Berkeley: University of California Press, 1985), pp. 303–14.
37. Freud's discussion of the Oedipus complex has several variations stemming from his claim that both genders have a bisexual component in their identity. All these versions however revolve around what he saw as the 'positive' case of the Oedipus complex resolution. On Mulvey's critical review of Freud's conception of femininity, see her 'Visual Pleasure'.
38. Sadism, according to Freud, originates in Thanatos (the death instinct, as opposed to Eros, the sexual libidinal instinct driving fetishization), which nevertheless merges into sexual instincts through which it is discharged.
39. For example, Freud, *Interpretation of Dreams*, p. 422, fn.1.
40. Mulvey, 'Visual Pleasure', p. 315, fn. 1.
41. Mulvey, 'Visual Pleasure', p. 315.
42. G. Studlar, 'Masochism and the Perverse Pleasures in the Cinema', in Bill Nichols (ed.), *Movies and Methods Vol. 2* (Berkeley: University of California Press, 1985), p. 605.
43. Studlar, 'Masochism', p. 605.
44. Mulvey, 'Visual Pleasure'.
45. Mary Ann Doane, 'Film and the Masquerade: Theorizing the Female Spectator', in *Screen*, 23 (1982), p. 81.
46. Doane, 'Film and the Masquerade', p. 78.
47. Doane, 'Film and the Masquerade', p. 87.
48. See Luce Irigaray, *This Sex Which Is Not One* (Ithaca, New York: Cornell University Press, 1985), p. 28.
49. Doane, 'Film and the Masquerade'.
50. Alexander Doty, 'Queer Theory', in J. Hill, P. C. Gibson, R. Dyer, E. A. Kaplan and P. Willemen (eds.), *The Oxford Guide to Film Studies* (Oxford: Oxford University Press, 1998), p. 148.
51. See Judith Butler, *Gender Trouble* (New York and London: Routledge, 1990).
52. Butler, *Gender Trouble*, p. 25.
53. Patricia White, 'Feminism and Film', in Hill et al., *The Oxford Guide to Film Studies*, p. 120.
54. White, 'Feminism and Film', p. 120.
55. In Richard Dyer's *Heavenly Bodies: Film Stars and Society* (British Film Institute, 1986), p. 18.
56. Stuart Hall, 'Encoding/Decoding', in S. Hall, D. Hobson, A. Lowe and P. Willis (eds.), *Culture, Media, Language* (London: Hutchinson Press, 1980), p. 138.
57. Doty, 'Queer Theory', p. 149.
58. White, 'Feminism and Film', p. 121.
59. Doty, Queer Theory, p. 151.
60. E.g. Chris Straayer, 'Redressing the "Natural": The Temporary Transvestite Film', in B. K. Grant (ed.), *Film Genre Reader II* (Austin: University of Texas Press, 1995), pp. 402–27.
61. Donna Haraway, 'A Cyborg Manifesto: Science, Technology, and Socialist-Feminism in the Late Twentieth Century', in *Simians, Cyborgs and Women: The Reinvention of Nature* (New York: Routledge, 1991), p. 149.
62. See Michael Heim, 'The Erotic Ontology of Cyberspace', in M. Benedikt (ed.), *Cyberspace: First Steps* (Cambridge, MA: The MIT Press, 1991), p. 61.

ANNOTATED GUIDE FOR FURTHER READING

I FROM THE PHOTOGENIC TO THE SIMULACRUM

Arnheim, R. (1957), *Film as Art*, Berkeley: University of California Press.

A Gestalt psychological approach to film that focuses on how films diverge from our visual perception of the real world.

Baudrillard, J. (1988), 'Simulacra and Simulations', in M. Poster (ed.), *Selected Writings*, Stanford: Stanford University Press.

In this seminal essay Baudrillard suggests that the distinction between the simulation and the simulated is arbitrary, masking the fact that they are both simulations without origin.

Bazin, A. (1967a), 'The Evolution of the Language of Cinema', in *What is Cinema? Volume I*, Berkeley: University of California Press.

The processes of film articulation should be aimed at conveying the beauty in nature's spatial depth, in its flowing temporality and in human existence.

Bazin, A. (1967b), 'The Ontology of the Photographic Image', in *What is Cinema? Volume I*, Berkeley: University of California Press.

The photograph, due to its unique way of reproduction, can reveal the world's beauty.

Liebman, S. E. (1983), *Jean Epstein's Early Film Theory, 1920–1922*, New York University Dissertation, Ann Arbor, MI: University Microfilms International.

In this dissertation Liebman offers a comprehensive and detailed exposition of Jean Epstein's film theory.

Michelson, A. (ed.) (1984), *Kino-Eye, the Writings of Dziga Vertov*, Berkeley: University of California Press.

A collection of Dziga Vertov's writings preceded by Michelson's excellent introduction that places Vertov's work in the context of Marxism and the constructivist movement.

Sobchack, V. (2000), 'At the Still Point of the Turning World' in V. Sobchack (ed.), *Meta-Morphing*, Minnesota: Minnesota University Press.

Sobchack explores the conception of change implied in morphing.

Tynjanov, Y. (1981), 'the Foundations of Cinema', in H. Eagle (ed.), *Russian Formalist Film Theory*, Ann Arbor: Michigan Slavic Publications.

Tynjanov argues here that cinematogenicity and montage are the two specific and unique aspects of the film medium that turn it into an art.

2 FILM CONSTRUCTS

Altman, R. (1995), 'A Semantic/Syntactic Approach to Film Genre', in B. K. Grant (ed.), *Film Genre Reader II*, Austin: University of Texas Press.

In this paper Altman suggests that 'the process of genre creation offers us not a single diachronic chart, but an always incomplete series of superimposed generic maps'.

Barthes, R. (1964), *Elements of Semiology*, New York: Hill and Wang.

Barthes offers an excellent brief exposition of structural linguistics and semiology that includes Barthes's own contribution to the field.

Barthes, R. (1972), 'Myth Today', *Mythologies*, Paris: Editions du Seuil.

Barthes here defines myths as articulations that naturalize ideologies.

Barthes, R. (1978), 'The Photographic Message', in *Image, Music, Text*, New York: Hill and Wang.

Barthes here discusses the 'photographic paradox' within a book whose thirteen essays offer semiological analyses of film, music and writing.

Bordwell, D. (1985), *Narration in the Fiction Film*, Madison, WI: University of Wisconsin Press.

The book offers a cognitive top-down model for the analysis of film narrative, style and viewing.

Carroll, N. (1988), *Mystifying Movies, Fads and Fallacies in Contemporary Film Theory*, New York: Columbia University Press.

A systematic dismantling of the Althusserian–Lacanian paradigm in film studies, with a counter-proposal of Carroll's own cognitivist film theory.

Lévi-Strauss, C. (1963), 'The Structural Study of Myth', in *Structural Anthropology*, New York: Basic Books Inc.

In this seminal article, Lévi-Strauss applies his structural method to the study of the different versions of the Oedipus myth.

Metz, C. (1976), 'On the Notion of Cinematographic Language', in Bill Nichols (ed.), *Movies and Methods*, Berkeley: University of California Press.

Metz claims here to have unearthed a unique film editing system based on arbitrary and conventional discrete units (syntagms) comprised of recurring combinations of film-specific signifiers (cuts, dissolves, wipes, etc.), through which the medium communicates time/space variations.

Neal, S. (1995), 'Questions of Genre', in B. K. Grant (ed.), *Film Genre Reader II*, Austin: University of Texas Press.

According to Neale, film genres are mixed, mutable and variable to begin with.

Schatz, T. (1995), 'The structural Influence: New Directions in Film Genre Study', in B. K. Grant (ed.), *Film Genre Reader II*, Austin: University of Texas Press.

Schatz suggests structuralism to be the most productive approach to genres.

Wollen, P. (1972a), 'The Auteur Theory', in *Signs and Meaning in the Cinema*, Bloomington, IN: Indiana University Press.

Wollen structurally overlaps upon the western genre's binary opposition of nature and civilization the work of prominent western film directors John Ford, Howard Hawks and Budd Boetticher.

Wollen, P. (1972b), 'The Semiology of the Cinema', *Signs and Meaning in the Cinema*, Bloomington, IN: Indiana University Press.

Wollen attempts a correction of Saussurean semiological approaches to film by importing Peirce's semiotics, dividing the medium into a documentary-indexical dimension, an iconic dimension and a symbolic-conventional dimension.

Wright, W. (1975), *Sixguns and Society*, Berkeley: California University Press.

Wright offers a structural study of the evolution of the western film in its sociopolitical context, focusing upon its shifting narrative configurations.

3 DIALECTIC FILM MONTAGE

Adorno, T. and Horkheimer, M. (1986), 'The Culture Industry: Enlightenment as Mass Deception', in *Dialectics of Enlightenment*, London: Verso.

In this seminal essay Adorno and Horkheimer argue that popular culture in the capitalist world is a culture industry pumping capitalist ideology into the exploited masses' minds.

Althusser, L. (1971), 'Ideology and Ideological State Apparatuses', in *Lenin and Philosophy*, New York: MRP.

Althusser suggests a clear and powerful explanation of how ideology persuades people, and how dominant ideologies form part of the state apparatus.

Baudry, J. L. (1985), 'Ideological Effects of the Basic Cinematographic Apparatus', in B. Nichols (ed.), *Movies and Methods Volume II*, Berkeley: University of California Press.

An Althusserian-inspired critique of film as an ideological apparatus.

Benjamin, W. (1969), 'The Work of Art in the Age of Mechanical Reproduction', in H. Arendt (ed.), *Illuminations*, New York: Shocken Books.

Film's reproducibility and jumpiness should be used to promote a Marxist revolution rather than produce a fake 'aura' for the brutal politics of fascism.

Eisenstein, S. M. (1949), 'A Dialectic Approach to Film Form', *Film Form*, New York: HBJ Books.

In this seminal article Eisenstein presents his dialectic montage doctrine exemplified mostly through an analysis of segments from his own films.

Heath, S. (1981), 'Narrative Space' in *Questions of Cinema*, Bloomington, IN: Indiana University Press.

Claiming that narrative films submit special compositions to action ('events take place'), Heath traces the ideologically driven evolution of narrative films from a neo-Marxist perspective while analysing alternatives.

Jameson, F. (1991), *Post-Modernism, Or, the Cultural Logic of Late Capitalism*, Durham, NC: Duke University Press.

Jameson critiques postmodern schizophrenia as symptom of late capitalism reification of emotions and aesthetic sensibilities.

MacBean, J. R. (1985), 'Vent d'est or Godard and Rocha at the Crossroads', in Bill Nichols (ed.), *Movies and Methods*, Berkeley: University of California Press.

MacBean discusses Godard's deconstruction of dominant film's manipulations of reality and beauty as against the loss of direction he finds in Glauber Rocha's filmmaking.

Michelson, A. (ed.) (1984), *Kino-Eye, the Writings of Dziga Vertov*, Berkeley: University of California Press.

A collection of Dziga Vertov's writings preceded by Michelson's excellent introduction that places Vertov's work in the context of Marxism and the constructivist movement.

Stam, R. and Spense, L. (1985), 'Colonialism, Racism, and Representation: An Introduction', in Bill Nichols (ed.), *Movies and Methods Vol. 2*, Berkeley: University of California Press.

Stam and Spense criticize the portrayals of the colonized in mainstream films while suggesting alternatives.

4 IMAGINARY SIGNIFIERS/VOYEURISTIC PLEASURES

Altman, C. F. (1985), 'Psychoanalysis and Cinema: The Imaginary Discourse', in Bill Nichols (ed.), *Movies and Methods Vol. 2*, Berkeley: University of California Press.

Altman critically surveys the 'film as dream' and 'film as mirror' metaphors used in psychoanalytic studies of film.

Butler, J. (1990), *Gender Trouble*, New York and London: Routledge.

Butler offers a definition of gender as performance rather than essence; as a diverse, split and shifting identity.

Dayan, D. (1976), 'The Tutor Code of Classical Cinema', in Bill Nichols (ed.), *Movies and Methods*, Berkeley: University of California Press.

Dayan's Lacanian psychoanalytical study analyses the shot–reverse-shot film constructs arguing that they suture the viewer's consciousness into the film.

Doane, M. A. (1982), 'Film and the Masquerade: Theorizing the Female Spectator', in *Screen*, 23: 74–88.

Doane suggests that by viewing femininity as masquerade female spectators can create a critical distance between the figuration of women in patriarchal films and their viewing it.

Doty, A. (1998), 'Queer Theory', in J. Hill, P. C. Gibson, R. Dyer, E. A. Kaplan and P. Willemen (eds.), *The Oxford Guide to Film Studies*, Oxford: Oxford University Press.

Doty offers an excellent introductory overview of the evolution of Queer studies and its major concerns.

Freud, S. (1965), *The Interpretation of Dreams*, New York: Avon Books.

In this extensive and fascinating study, Freud advances through many examples his thesis that dreams are a major venue allowing individuals to relieve themselves of repressed impulses and wishes without threatening their well-being and their mental equilibrium.

Hall, S. (1980), 'Encoding/Decoding', in S. Hall, D. Hobson, A. Lowe and P. Willis (eds.), *Culture, Media, Language*, London: Hutchinson Press.

Hall's groundbreaking article identifies in the process of communication how the producer's 'encoding' of a message undergoes changes in its 'decoding' by the receiver.

Haraway, D. (1991), 'A Cyborg Manifesto: Science, Technology, and Socialist-Feminism in the Late Twentieth Century', in *Simians, Cyborgs and Women: The Reinvention of Nature*, New York: Routledge.

Haraway explores the revolutionary potential of the hybrid machine/organism cyborg myth.

Lacan, J. (1977), 'The Mirror Stage as Formative of the Function of the I', in *Ecrits, a Selection*, New York: W.W. Norton and Company.

Lacan's seminal thesis deals with infants' first notion of self as resulting from their identifying themselves as whole and coordinated in their mirror reflection.

Metz, C. (1985), 'Story/Discourse: Notes on Two Kinds of Voyeurism', in Bill Nichols (ed.), *Movies and Methods Vol. 2*, Berkeley: University of California Press.

Metz argues here that the film's inducement of the mirror stage in viewers positions them as peeping Toms in relation to films, where actors behave as if nobody is watching them.

Mulvey, L. (1985), 'Visual Pleasure and Narrative Cinema', in Bill Nichols (ed.), *Movies and Methods Vol. 2*, Berkeley: University of California Press.

In this groundbreaking article Mulvey suggests that mainstream filmmaking reflects the 'patriarchal unconscious', replicating and reinforcing through its modes of articulation and gender figurations patterns that discriminate against women.

Mulvey, L. (1989), 'Afterthoughts on "Visual Pleasure and Narrative Cinema" inspired by King Vidor's *Duel in the Sun*', in *Visual and Other Pleasures*, London: Macmillan.

Mulvey argues that female spectators may identify with the male protagonist in its representing their repressed freedom of ego.

Straayer, C. (1995), 'Redressing the "Natural": The Temporary Transvestite Film', in B. K. Grant (ed.), *Film Genre Reader II*, Austin: University of Texas Press.

Construing films dealing with transvestism as a genre, Straayer analyses the genre's rhetorical strategies.

INDEX